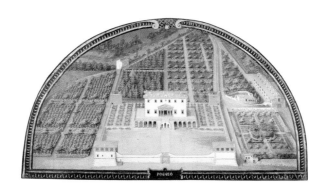

Villas of Tuscany

Villas
of Tuscany

Text by
Carlo Cresti

Photographs by
Massimo Listri

VENDOME

First published in the United States in 2003 by
The Vendome Press
1334 York Avenue
New York, NY 10021

Library of Congress Cataloging-in-Publication Data
Cresti, Carlo.
  [Civiltà delle Ville Toscane. English]
  Villas of Tuscany / text by Carlo Cresti; photographs by
Massimo Listri.-- Rev.ed.
    p.cm.
Includes bibliographical references and index.
 ISBN 0-86565-243-0 (alk. paper)
 1. Architecture, Domestic--Italy--Tuscany. I. Listri,
Massimo. II. Title
NA7594.C7413 2003
728.8'0945'5--dc22

                    2003057561

ISBN: 0-86565-243-0

Printed in Italy

CONTENTS

An Architecture in a Constructed Landscape

"Man makes the place, and the place makes the man."

Tuscan proverb

Several well-known discussions of Florentine and Tuscan villas begin by referring to Giovanni Boccaccio's descriptions of such architecture in the *Decameron*, a popular reference often cited to show that the villa can boast an ancient and noble ancestry. In effect, however, the villa has no need of evocative origins or worthy precedents, for when it first appeared, at the end of the 15th century, the villa was already in itself a type of architecture with a distinctive, and therefore noble, character.

Those who try to identify the villa's illustrious antecedents in Boccaccio's work generally overlook the fact that the place he describes was probably an exaggerated idealization of an "island of deliverance," a sort of earthly paradise created by the imagination of the narrator and likely to have been far removed from reality. This seems logical enough, given the appalling conditions that must have prevailed in Florence during the plague year 1348.

With the selfish but understandable desire to "spurn and flee the realms of hell and its trappings," the thoughtless young protagonists of the *Decameron* decided to leave the city with their servants for the countryside in search of "that festivity, good cheer, and pleasure" which the rural areas seemed to hold "without in any way exceeding the limits of reason."

And so Boccaccio's band of fugitives from "sadness" reached a place "no farther than two brief miles" from the city, located "above a modest hill that was just as far removed from our roads and lush with saplings and plants with green fronds that were pleasant to observe. At the top of the hill there was a palace with a large and handsome courtyard, and loggias, chambers, and rooms, all of which were beautiful and filled with gay and decorative paintings, and surrounded by meadows and wondrous gardens where fountains of the coolest water flowed. . . ."

Here "the young people, accompanied by lovely women, and thinking delightful thoughts," entertained themselves by weaving "beautiful garlands," playing the lute and the viola, and amorously singing "sweet and cheerful songs." Here, they sat in a ring at the center of a "meadow where the grass was green and long."

The allegorical aspects, stemming from the notion of a "profane" Garden of Eden, are clear enough and can be found as well in a number of contemporary paintings. However, both there and in the prose representation drawn by Boccaccio, the identification of the image with an actual villa would appear to be a tenuous possibility at best.

The Boccaccian setting does not change even when the happy troupe, "murmuring, bantering, and laughing," arrived at "a peak, filled with green herbs and flowers," where another "beautiful and costly palace stood." This second palace was also composed of "large halls," "clean and ornate chambers entirely furnished with everything a room requires," "spacious and cheerful courtyards," and "a loggia overlooking the whole courtyard." Next to the "palace" lay a garden "that was surrounded by a wall" with wide, vine-covered pathways. The sides of these pathways were "almost enclosed by trellises laden with white and crimson roses and jasmine," and in the middle of a meadow stood "a fountain of the whitest marble with marvelous inlay work" crowned by a "statue" borne upon column.

The Boccaccian garden of delights also contained "one hundred kinds of pleasing animals," allowing the merry band to watch as "rabbits bounded into view, hares scampered away, and roebuck rested peacefully, while their fawns grazed nearby." Then, symptomatically, the young people gathered "around the beautiful fountain" to sing, dance, and partake of "fine and delicate victuals."

The walled garden, a safely protected earthly paradise that Boccaccio had previously described in nearly identical terms in his *Amorosa visione,* is a symbolic microcosm whose internal *topoi*—the rose, the vine, the arbor, the fountain, the water, the jasmine, and the deer—represent almost excessively transparent allegories of regeneration, immortality, purification, youth, and fertility.

As a reflection of ancient Classical doctrine, this *hortus conclusus* may therefore be regarded as the expression of an ideology meant to transform a rarefied and metaphorical scene into an occasion of quasi-initiatory rituals, moments of contemplation, and intellectual games preparatory to erotic play. At the same time, however, the generic "palace," being endowed with a courtyard, rooms, and a loggia, does not provide much fuel for imaginative interpretation. Thus, to search for an archetypal villa in Boccaccio's hint of a building would be misguided, to say the least. At most, we might infer that the location of the structure on the top of a hill and not far from the city conveys a general conception of how a "gentleman's residence" in the country would have been sited.

It would be equally futile to hark back to the description of the villa in *Tifernium* by Pliny the Younger (another author often needlessly disturbed by those seeking primary sources) in the hope of proving that the Tuscan villa originated in Imperial Rome.

Giovanni Villani, who had just completed his *Cronica* when Boccaccio began work on the *Decameron*, tried to draw a historical analogy by noting that "there was not a citizen rich or poor who had not or would not build large and sumptuous dwellings and possessions in the country." As a result, Villani continued, visitors arriving in Florence "believed that the number of impressive buildings and gorgeous palaces that stood as far as three miles from the city were all built in the Roman way." But even in this case, the reference to Rome must be interpreted as a proud and celebratory recollection of a brilliant and ennobling "Caesarian" model (to which the foundation of the Florentine Colony was usually traced), capable of serving as confirmation of the "nobility and grandeur" of medieval Florence, which had indeed become one of the most important financial centers in Europe.

The "impressive buildings and gorgeous palaces" in the suburbs recalled by Villani do not, however, provide sufficient evidence for

Jacopo del Sellaio, The Banquet of Ahaserus (Uffizi, Florence). In this pictorial allegory, the themes of palace and walled garden—courtyard, loggia, fountain, grapevines, and fawn—have been treated in a manner consistent with descriptions found in Boccaccio's Decameron.

the identification of a specific prototype, nor do they add any significant information to what may be considered the "prehistoric phase" of the Tuscan villa.

The rise of the villa as a cultural and formal entity occurred over time and in parallel with the ancient customs of the Tuscan patriarchy. For a more realistic sense of that process, we should probably trust the words of Anton Francesco Doni, writing in the latter half of the 16th century. As a reliable, first-hand witness to the phenomenon of the villa, which had just emerged in its primary architectural expression, Doni abandoned rhetoric, went straight to the heart of the matter, and summarized the evolution of the country residence from the initial "artisan's property" (i.e., a purely functional abode) to the patrician dwelling (a residence suitable for a family of rank and a place for pleasure and relaxation). This was an architectural and stylistic evolution that unfolded in tandem with the growing prosperity of the Tuscan family, gradually manifesting itself through an often random assemblage of generally favored structural elements, among them courtyards, loggias, and dovecotes.

"The construction of such homes," Doni wrote, "is without any model whatsoever, given that a room for the summer might have been built by the grandfather, a stable for the horse built perhaps by the great-grandfather, or the dovecote constructed by an old grandmother with a penchant for pigeons. An oven, a shed, and an extra garret give a poor house the appearance of a rich one, with its elm tree along the road to provide shade, with the chattering of its farmhands and a neighbor to pass the time."

Once we can see how the stables and other subsidiary buildings gave way to drawing rooms, bedrooms, and such, it becomes possible to make a credible reconstruction of the progressive stages through which the villa came into being. In other words, as feudalism evolved into a bourgeois landholding system, it encouraged the transformation of the lordly manor—*la casa da signore*—into the villa, which emerged bit by bit as the owner modified his farmhouse to accord with his desires and ambitions.

At a time when the *casa da signore* still lacked a clear architectural identity, and even later, when such an identity had been established, the patriarchal system constituted a steady, ongoing factor within the development of the Tuscan villa. It must not be forgotten that the farm-estate, owing to the metayage, or share-cropper, system common throughout the Tuscan countryside, was organized along the lines of the family. The rural home acquired the connotation of a *casa da signore*, which then became a place of mediation between agrarian and urban cultures, inasmuch as the fortunes of the owner and his family became more and more linked with those of the land, at the same time that the owner's family rose to greater social status, thereby taking an ever-more crucial part in the urbanization of the countryside.

The farmhouse-villa was thus converted into the palace-villa, because the primary need to supervise work in the fields gradually became involved with or even subordinate to the

subsequent desire for a holiday passed in idle contemplation of life in the countryside. This occurred because the family, in the interests of their growing ambition, assumed a deciding role in the aggrandizement of their house, with each successive generation modifying or adding something of its own to the ancestral holding. Consequently, every *paterfamilias-*

whether a relatively modest bourgeois or a Grand Duke–charged his heirs with the task of continuing and consolidating the work of the past, which brought constant enhancement of the dwelling itself and a reinforcement of the sense that it represented a particular family.

To paraphrase the words of Guglielmo Ferrero, we should perhaps try to discover the villa's invisible "genes" in the authority, intelligence, foresight, and experience of the founding fathers–that is, in the "principles of legitimacy" that would govern the villa's destiny throughout the centuries to come.

Leon Battista Alberti made similar observations, and, as a Humanist who rejected communal forms of life, he claimed that, for

Giovanni di Paolo, Madonna of Humility (detail; Pinacoteca Nazionale, Siena). The landscape in the background is an accurate representation of the Tuscan countryside, with its geometrically sectioned fields and great diversity of crops.

secular purposes, the family represented the best social structure. Believing the emotive and hereditary bonds that tied the household together to be conceptually both solid and valid, Alberti maintained that any behavior and investments serving to benefit the family were justifiable. For this quintessential Renaissance man, the family should regard the increase in their fame and honor within society as a determining purpose, treating it indeed as the ultimate principle behind their every action.

In his *Famiglia*, moreover, Alberti urged that privilege be granted to private rather than public interests, viewing the flow of material goods and ideas towards the countryside as a major defense against the roguery committed by "scoundrels in the city." The serenity of the soul and the fruits of the soil offered by a country estate represented an enticing alternative, with the villa viewed as "above all

grateful, reliable, and true" because "no envy, hatred, or evil can arise in the hearts of those who till the soil."

However, the bourgeois villa as a type distinguishable by its architectural qualities arrived only after the patriarchal feeling had become distilled through a growing phenomenon known as the diversification of investment, which, in this instance, meant the conversion of liquid wealth derived from urban pursuits (trading, banking, manufacturing) into the illiquid wealth of property in the country, soon to be deemed a status symbol as well as a repository of material well-being. Now the villa would represent the tangible manifestation of power that every lord and landowner expected to possess and display. Quite simply, it constituted an essential rung on the socioeconomic ladder, a conclusive link, expressed through architectural form, in a long

and complex chain of social relations whose aim was to reinforce traditional privilege. The villa, in brief, would become the ultimate sign and instrument of prestige.

The colonization of the farmhouse by the mercantile bourgeoisie triggered the final dismemberment of the old feudal landholding system, with the simultaneous consequence that it added fresh impetus to the urbanization of the countryside.

This led to an overall structural reorganization of Tuscan lands, which had already been significantly altered by the human presence. Increasingly, the countryside assumed an "artificial" or "constructed" quality, losing its pristine nature as a result of interventions that changed its topographical appearance and the very nature of the soil itself.

Pictorial representations from the era bear witness to the geometrical division of the land,

the regularity of its cultivated fields, and the orderly patterns of roads, paths, ditches, and hedgerows.

The plains plowed into parallel furrows, the borders of fields marked out by fences or rows of trees, the meticulously straight lines within vineyards, the embankments and terraces that divided up the hills and slopes, and the rock walls that supported them formed the "sublime embroidery" described by Emilio Sereni. Against this richly detailed background stood the substantial farmhouses with their vegetable plots, small farmsteads scattered among the hills, tiny hamlets and villages, and here and there a castle perched upon a rocky outcrop proudly dominating all it surveyed.

Landscape elements of feudal times mixed with those of the new urban society, as a network of communication arose between the town within its circle of high defense walls and

Gherardo Starnina, The Hermitage (Uffizi, Florence). An abstract variation on its theme, this painting shows nature enchantingly transformed by architectural outcroppings (churches and castles), infrastructures (bridges), and humble cottages.

the peripheral areas without, where a dense mesh of minor constructions served to mediate between city and country.

Tuscans in general, whether rich or poor, like to personalize the land and leave their own mark upon it. They enjoy discovering "reminders" along the routes through valleys and over hills. They feel reassured by finding landmarks that distinguish important crossroads and record the progress of their journey. Tuscans, in short, like to annotate the vast book of nature with their own signifying commentaries, thereby giving proof of their individual creativity.

In this way Tuscany acquired the characteristics that are so familiar today: rows of tall, dark, slender cypresses, silver-gray olive trees bordering the sunken roads running deep between narrow rock walls, farmhouses flanked by stables and haylofts, manor houses with gardens, small roadside shrines, chapels, and churches. These "constructed" elements were not intended to merge imperceptibly into the environment, but rather to define the relationship between culture and nature.

In this landscape, the villa–or, more precisely, any building that is comparable even if not identical in type–appears as an emerging point of reference and a dominant element in the plains and hills. It becomes the terminal focus of a road, the often-isolated nucleus of smaller holdings, the welding point or hinge that connects the different parts of the countryside, the sign of inhabited space in a region defined–and not by chance–as a "land of cities."

Thus, Goro Dati was right when, in his description of the Florentine landscape, written between the end of the 14th century and the beginning of the 15th, he observed that "outside the walls of the city there are wonderful residences of the citizenry with ornate gardens of marvelous beauty, and the countryside is so rich in palaces and noble residences and so crowded with citizens that it resembles a city; filled with an infinite number of castles. . . ."

In his *Laudatio Fiorentinae Urbis* of 1405, Leonardo Bruni expressed the very same views.

From the City Palace
to the Country Palace

Among the isolated clusters of dwellings so characteristic of the Tuscan countryside there gradually ceased to be much difference between the traditional fortified castle with its feudal associations and the newer, nonmilitary residence required by a proto-Renaissance *signor*. This evolution occurred because the conditions of life had altered to the point where the old battlemented castle, which once existed to defend the terrain and provide a safe haven in case of need, could shed its martial qualities for those of a seasonal residence designed for rest and recreation in the country.

In the course of the evolution from castle to villa there were also several intermediate steps marked by the appearance of the country house *da signore* and the suburban *palazzetto*. While the overall sampling may appear limited, it nonetheless includes certain uncodifiable types of dwellings that, with a kind of spontaneous

empiricism, add to the miscellany of distinctive elements, along with those of economic or environmental circumstance and personal or family life-style.

The *casa da signore*, more or less modest in size, usually resulted from a process designed to enlarge and embellish an existing and scenically situated *casa da contadino* or "peasant dwelling." Successive building campaigns would have turned it into a comfortable, aristocratic residence, where the owner could keep an eye on the operations of his estate while simultaneously indulging himself in the pleasures of the country.

In the suburban *palazzetto*, on the other hand, many of its urban features were gradually softened by elements that had originated in the villa, including, for example, the garden, a substitute for the orchard. With the diminution of both its defensive purpose and its function as

Villa Medici La Petraia, as represented in a land-survey drawing of 1697 (State Archives, Florence). Here, the villa clearly dominates the surrounding countryside.

a "center of cultivation," the palazzetto outside the town walls gained importance, in ways both practical and superstructural, as a domain conducive to delightful living.

Indeed, some of the fortress-villas, such as the Medician residences of Cafaggiolo (replete with internal moats, according to Vasari) and Il Trebbio, or the small peripheral fortified palaces on the order of Careggi, had, in the first half of the 15th century, to camouflage their original military elements (towers, crenellations, galleried sentry paths along the tops of walls) in order to appear more suited to their new role as places of leisure. Careggi, for example, had a small, airy loggia added on the *piano nobile*, or main floor.

If we analyze examples from a selection of the intermediate types of country residence, we are confronted with a miscellany of ground plans and combinations of volumes that in no way lend themselves to systematic classification. The buildings in question appear as an assortment of disparate structures, some with old towers and others without, and all different in height as well as in the date and techniques of their construction. The majority of them are blocky constructions with openings pierced in an irregular and seemingly arbitrary manner, a sign of their previous service as farmhouses. Sections added on at a later date are usually enhanced by central or corner loggias and by windows framed in stone, evidence not only of formal concerns but also of a desire for prestigious connotation. Many of these dwellings are arranged about courtyards of limited dimensions, not always centrally placed and sometimes not even arcaded on all sides. The absence of symmetry and the casualness that mark these haphazard assemblies of various parts are perhaps the only constant of such buildings.

Perhaps none of these various building components could be called specifically Tuscan, since the loggia and the courtyard, for instance, derive from an ancient Mediterranean tradition, while the dovecote tower existed in other parts of Italy. Indeed, during this period, no stylistic innovations or local peculiarities

appeared in the country houses of Tuscany. What truly distinguished such dwellings from those of other regions was frugality, a characteristic that appears to have guided the architectural aspirations of the entire Florentine nobility.

In regard to Classical influence, none seems to have affected the Tuscan villa before the mid-15th century, other than a vague longing for the seductive myth of the "wholesomeness of rural life." And even this did not figure among the motivations that yielded architectural projects.

The Medici villas of Careggi (described by Galeazzo Maria Sforza, with excessive enthusiasm, as "a most beautiful palace") and Belcanto (at Fiesole) are interesting examples of this indifference to Classical models. In both houses the building campaigns carried out by Michelozzo (between 1450 and 1460) consisted

Villa Medici at Cafaggiolo, as seen in a detail from a lunette fresco by Giusto Utens (Museo di Firenze com'era, Florence).

IL TREBBIO

Villa Medici Il Trebbio,
depicted in a lunette fresco
by Giusto Utens (Museo di
Firenze com'era, Florence).

of adaptations of the existing structures, an operation dictated by practical necessity and limited means, not by Roman models known through Latin literature. At Villa di Belcanto, the entrance portico (the only "architectural feature" of this modest abode) cannot be considered an imitative or revivalist attempt to create a formal vestibule in the antique manner (*al modo e all'usanza antica*). Moreover, the stepped terracing of the grounds was surely a practical solution to the hilly terrain rather than an effort to re-create the legendary garden described by Pliny the Younger, which was furnished with avenues, a hippodrome, a covered gallery, a ball court, a semicircular seat, and a pool.

In other words, the architecture of the first Medici villas had yet to reflect the Humanist canons already standard in the public and private buildings of Florence.

Before aesthetic factors prevailed over practical considerations–before, that is, the patrician villa became to all intents and purposes the concrete expression of its owner's cultural aims and ambitions–there was an interval of several years during which only the imagination of refined philosophers and poets, such as Marsilio Ficino and Angelo Poliziano, could conjure up the abstract idea of a villa that lent itself to such a pursuit. In this the leading members of the Florentine Humanist circle were returning to the concept of intellectual leisure eulogized by Seneca, Varrone, Martial, Cato, and Columella.

We should not forget that, depending on the life-style of the patron, the villa was essentially a manifestation of a conservative nature. At the same time, it was also an indication of the economic prestige and social rank of the family, subject, even more than the palace in the city, to the vicissitudes of power and fashion.

True enough, the country palace materialized a desire to escape from city life, but it also embodied clear analogies with its urban counterpart. The replication of the palatial in the country came somewhat slowly because the patron had to be certain that any investment in the accessory aspects of his villa would yield a profitable social or even political "return." Meanwhile, he had also to obtain the collaboration of an architect equipped with the right experience.

Despite the potential freedom of architectural intervention seemingly offered by an isolated country house, the grandiose elements of urban *palazzi* assumed a decidedly prosaic quality once they appeared in the rural villa. It was as if they had undergone adaptation in order to fit in with the reality of the bucolic environment. Meanwhile, the façade of the villa, like that of the town palace, still tended to eschew an ostentatious show of wealth and social standing.

The villa did not, therefore, constitute a modest double of the palace in the city, but, rather, something comparable yet different. It could be seen as a product of intellectual and patriarchal reasoning, which understood how to distinguish compatible roles, social levels, and purposes, to such a degree that if a country villa had been transported into an urban context, its unmistakable and immutable "rurality" would have become immediately self-evident.

Even a large imposing residence like the Medici's Poggio a Caiano exhibited a certain

awkwardness, together with an undeniable elegance meant, beginning in 1485, to express the needs of a culturally aware and demanding patron. The heavy box-like upper structure may seem to crush the ground-floor arcades, but the villa as a whole leaves no doubt about its having been constructed to dominate and govern the surrounding countryside.

A perfect reflection of the Humanist leanings of Lorenzo the Magnificent, Poggio a Caiano was the first building erected from scratch in which it is possible to recognize the attributes proper to the villa. In other words, the history of the Tuscan villa was born with the princely residence of Poggio a Caiano, which bears many characteristics derived from its genesis, including a number of limitations.

The fact that it has always seemed imperative to view Laurentian Poggio a Caiano as the absolute archetype of the Tuscan villa may explain why such pains had been taken to nurture the myth surrounding its construction,

even to the point of distorting supposedly objective analyses of the architectural result and its relevance.

Part of the myth concerns the "clear" role played by the ideas of Leon Battista Alberti in preparing the way for the Laurentian villa, a role adduced from Alberti's dedication of *De re aedificatoria* to Il Magnifico. Also important to the myth is the Classical origin of certain formal components found at Poggio, as well as the conviction that the villa was the first Tuscan example of a building that courageously "opens itself" to the landscape.

As for the first contention, it has to be said that Poggio–that Laurentian "palace in the country"—owes nothing to Alberti for the notion that the heart of the house should lie in the central courtyard, around which "gravitate all the minor parts, as if towards a public square at the center of the building." Admittedly, Lorenzo the Magnificent must have been aquainted with Alberti's treatise even before the Florentine edition of 1485. Meanwhile, however, the Medici's Villa Careggi already possessed an inner courtyard, which afforded Il Magnifico ample opportunity to judge the advantages and disadvantages of the arrangement. As a result, perhaps, he deferred not to the great Humanist theoretician but, instead, followed a personal whim (as Vasari attests) and assigned the project to Giuliano da Sangallo, who proposed a central salon instead of a courtyard. It would therefore seem that Lorenzo did not wholeheartedly embrace the authority of Classicism as re-examined by Alberti in *De re aedificatoria*. On the contrary, it would seem that by adopting the proposals offered by Sangallo–especially the ennobling pediment on the façade–Il Magnifico favored an imitative use of antique forms as a means of enhancing contemporary architecture. It should not therefore surprise that the celebrated triangular pediment at Poggio a Caiano looks as if it had been grafted on artificially, an ostentatious and anachronistic feature serving to emphasize more than camouflage the surrounding, rather banal arrangement of modest, traditional Florentine

View of the 16th-century palazzo di campagna, painted by Alessandro del Barbiere on the vault of a room in Villa Corsi at Sesto Fiorentino.

19

This detail from a 16th-century Florentine tapestry by Benedetto Squilli (from a cartoon by Giovanni Stradano) shows Lorenzo the Magnificent following the progress of construction work on his villa at Poggio a Caiano (Depositi delle Gallerie, Florence).

windows. Probably the Poggio a Caiano pediment, together with its temple-like portico (sometimes attributed to Etruscan models), should be viewed as an evocative fragment (almost like a prefiguration of post-modernism) placed within a context to which it was not entirely suited. Or again, it could be seen as the realization of a "whim," the fruit of an impromptu inspiration on the part of the patron (a lover of architecture) or even the designer. Finally, it may well represent a compromise between early ambition and later moderation.

Many well-known scholars have seen Classical influence clearly at work in the *basis villae*, the large arcaded substructure at Villa di Poggio a Caiano. The arcades surrounding Pompei's Villa of the Mysteries (Marchini, Heydenreich) and the basements of the Temple of Jupiter at Terracina (Foster, Bardazzi-Castellani), the Temple of Fortuna Primigenia at Palestrina, and the Temple of Claudius at

Rome have all been put forth as possible antecedents. So far, however, no one has dared to suggest that the arcades at the base of Poggio a Caiano might have sprung from more prosaic sources than the noble and antique ones so consistently proposed. For example, it may have seemed advisable to raise the living quarters of the residence a few meters higher relative to the surrounding countryside, where the River Ombrone often overflowed its banks, creating swampy conditions conducive to malaria. In Lorenzo the Magnificent's time the cause of this disease was attributed to miasmatic air; thus, raising the villa higher above the ground would have also exposed it to healthy breezes. In fact, the whole area around Poggio a Caiano was distinctly malarial, its manifold rice paddies serving as a breeding ground for mosquitoes. We should remember (thanks to Pieraccini) that Francesco I de' Medici and Bianca Cappello died at Poggio a

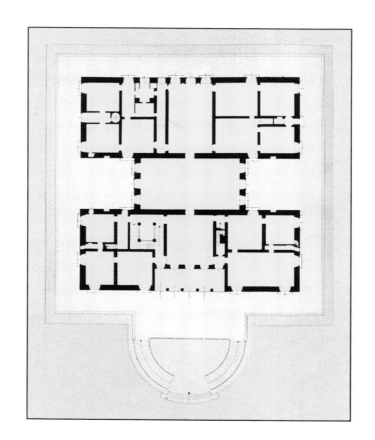

Plan of the piano nobile at Villa Medici, Poggio a Caiano.

Caiano in October 1587 from "malarial tertian fever."

Lastly, there is the often cited "openness" of Villa Poggio a Caiano towards the outside world, a famous attribute that one should admit is somewhat imaginary, all things considered. No doubt the continuous balustraded terrace provided splendid panoramic views from all four sides, just as the original high galleries on two of the lateral façades must have given wonderful visual access to the ambient landscape. However, it is equally certain that the tall arcaded basement kept the locals at a comfortable and seemly distance from the princely residence, thereby reducing the possibility of immediate and organic contact with the surrounding terrain. Moreover, one has only to note the scarcity and modest dimensions of the windows and doorways to realize just how cautiously Villa di Poggio a Caiano opened itself to the external environment.

The placement of the villa's central salon between the front and rear blocks is original, but it also presents some problems. Here, the salon serves as both an impressive public reception hall and a passage to and from the villa's two parallel wings, rather like the situation in Venetian palaces, where a *portego* or corridor flanked by paired series of rooms cuts across the entire depth of the building to the opposite façade. But while two of the *portego*'s four sides could boast glazed walls with openwork balconies, yielding a sense of interaction between the interior and the main canal on one side and a small courtyard or secondary canal on the other, the central salon of Villa di Poggio a Caiano was much less fortunate, thanks to its not being part of an urban building. As a result, the room has to make do, at its two extremities, with meager tripartite openings (each a central door-window flanked by two windows raised and rescaled like those of other rooms), whose view upon the world outside is then "blinkered" by the projecting walls of the long front and rear wings.

One should not forget that once Poggio a Caiano had been completed, the patron thought it best to surround the villa, at a discreet distance, with a high wall, another impediment to "openness."

Despite all these factors, the mistaken conviction that Poggio a Caiano represents the concrete or ideal reference point for other Florentine or Tuscan villas still flourishes. Not even the distinctive H plan of Il Magnifico's new country palace would ever be adopted for subsequent villas built in Tuscany. And rather than too elitist, the layout was merely thought to be impractical and awkward, inasmuch as the centrally placed salon split the building in two, both horizontally and vertically.

Going beyond the myth, we can say that while Poggio a Caiano may constitute the first realization in Tuscany of a specific building

POGGIO

Villa Medici at Poggio a Caiano, in a bird's-eye view painted by Giusto Utens (Museo di Firenze com'era, Florence).

style, the villa does not bear out the claims for its having served as a model that inspired widespread imitation. It therefore remains a problematic *unicum*, something unique, difficult to understand, and hard to interpret.

Still, one thing remains certain: Villa di Poggio a Caiano is an emblematic product from the Laurentian age. Although defined as

golden," the period actually witnessed a substantial decline in both the quality and the character of Florentine architecture. It was an era when mediocre designers such as Maiano and honest, unpretentious craftsmen such as Giuliano da Sangallo could achieve great success.

Types and Styles
of the Villa

Baldassarre Peruzzi's U-shaped plan–which the architect had employed in 1505 for the Roman villa of Agostino Chigi, later called "La Farnesina," as well as for Villa Le Volte built for Sigismondo Chigi near Siena–enjoyed limited success in Tuscany.

Breaking away from the classic block-shaped building erected around a closed inner courtyard, Peruzzi offered a new and modern approach. The villa would now open out by means of two lateral wings set at right angles to the main body, which extended their arms almost as if to embrace the surrounding countryside. The section of the building between the wings also broke free, once Peruzzi placed an open portico on the ground floor with a matching loggia directly above it.

The Peruzzian-type buildings of the 16th century that conform more or less to this plan are Villa I Collazzi, Villa Tatttoli alla Romola, the Gioiello at Pian de' Giullari, the northern prospect of the Medici villa of Pratolino, and Lappeggi. Then from the 17th century there are Villa Gerini at Montughi (now demolished) and Villa Cetinale near Siena. None of the Florentine villas mentioned, however, exhibits Peruzzi's elegant "scoring" of façades articulated by orders of pilasters, projecting stringcourses, and the characteristic *fascia* or "band" under the eaves punctuated by the small windows of the attic floor. Peruzzi's stylistic innovations–which, in the eyes of Florentine patrons and architects, no doubt suffered from the defect of having been inspired by Rome and of coming from the enemy Siena (which was conquered by Florence only in 1555)–did enjoy some success in Florence (the Pitti Palace being the most notable example). However, it was not enough to change the fixed mentality and traditions of the Florentine ruling class,

Villa Le Volte near Siena, in a drawing from the 18th century (Vatican Library).

Giuseppe Zocchi, View of Villa I Collazzi, from Vedute delle ville e d'altri luoghi della Toscana (Florence, 1744).

Giuseppe Zocchi, View of Villa Gerini at Montughi, from Vedute delle ville e d'altri luoghi della Toscana (Florence, 1744).

although the Mannerist Buontalenti had himself introduced, with some modifications, U-shaped façades in the Medici villas of Pratolino (1569) and Lappeggi (1585).

During the 16th century the Florentine villa remained faithful to the well-tried block layout, and it was in fact Buontalenti, principal architect of the Medici villas, who persevered with the closed-volume style, which now risked becoming a monotonous stereotype, devoid of spatial interest. The superficial geometric rigor of the building mass, the essential functionalism, the so-called "Classical restraint" (or "Etruscan sobriety"), the cautious use of materials, the sameness of the façades–these hid the lack of three-dimensional fantasy in the Buontalenti villas (a fantasy that the architect was allowed to express only when he designed settings for court entertainments).

The refusal to abandon this compact though banal architectural design emphasized the separation of the villa from nature–later made up for by the literally fabulous gardens, which pulsed with metaphors, analogies, and Classical symbolism.

Perhaps Buontalenti's inspiration for Artimino (1594) came from the villa of Montepò at Scansano (1548), which is characterized by four fortified corner towers, and the solution tried at the villa of Serravezza (1565) with its corner bastions, elements that must have appealed to one who was a military architect by profession.

For Pratolino, apart from the obvious Peruzzian influence and the very sophisticated layout of the garden, Buontalenti designed a massive building that consists of three cubic blocks fitted together in the shape of the letter T.

Nothing is known of the architect who worked at Ambrogiana (1587), a villa immediately recognizable by its four towers. Even here the architectural style is not wholly original, for a similar installation had already been adopted at Villa Niccolini (1568), Camugliano di Pisa, and at Villa Bernardini (1540), Coselli, near Lucca.

In fact, the country residences of the Grand Dukes of Tuscany, despite their being symbols of wealth and power, do not represent attractive examples of stylistic innovation (other than in their gardens). And if they failed to be imitated, it was certainly not because rich Tuscans wished to avoid the embarrassment of constructing villas that might in any way emulate those of their Grand Dukes.

There does exist, on the other hand, an undoubted correspondence between the consolidation of the Medici government and the construction of the grand-ducal villas throughout Tuscany. Its political aspect (that is, the visible presence of the prince of the territory) does not altogether succeed in concealing a certain competitive snobbishness with regard to the other Renaissance courts in Europe, together with a desire to return to the land. The latter might be seen as a proud, self-celebratory homage to the remote rural origins of the Cafaggiolo stock and the affirmation of a continuous patriarchal line.

Some of the many grand-ducal villas functioned as strategic observation posts close by a state border (for example, the one at Serravezza), while others were located near

Francesco I de' Medici and court functionaries in the villa garden at Pratolino, as portrayed by the sculptor Giambologna in a relief made of gold on an amethyst ground (Museo degli Argenti, Florence).

important centers of production (marble quarries and silver smelting works). Some functioned as administrative centers for agricultural, fishing, or land-reclamation activities (Monte Vettolini, Cerreto Guidi, and Coltano), and still others (Colle Salvetti, Ambrogiana) were places to stay during the long grand-ducal progresses through the various parts of Tuscany. Last of all, there were the villas—and these formed the majority—that served as large, comfortable hunting lodges (for example, Poggio a Caiano, Artimino, La Magia, and Ambrogiana), or simply as places for enjoyment, such as Pratolino.

The diversification and interchangeability of the villas' roles, ranging from official state duties to recreational pleasures, seem proof of a shrewd utilization of circumstances and contingencies rather than of a rational, well-organized program. It is difficult to see in such differentiation, in the often seemingly whimsical siting (perhaps following the migration of game) of these scattered palaces, a systematic project planned and realized for the

political and economic management of the territory (as some scholars have suggested), a project that was, on the other hand, more or less explicit in the contemporary distribution of villas in the Veneto.

Florence and Tuscany, of course, had no architect with the genius of Palladio. This is yet another reason why the monotonous country residences of the Medici Grand Dukes, which differed from those of other aristocratic families only in size, confirm the absence of a specific and original architectural type that could be called the Medicean villa.

Let us not, however, make the common mistake of imagining that the villas of the Medici represent the architectural reality for the whole of Tuscany. We have seen how Peruzzi managed, practically with a single construction, to create a stylistic controversy in the Florentine region. During the 16th century the architecture of Sienese villas, with its original and daring solutions, moved further and further away from the clichés dominant in the area around Florence. Just one architectural

Villa Medici L'Ambrogiana at Montelupo Fiorentino, in a lunette fresco painted by Giusto Utens (Museo di Firenze com'era, Florence).

26

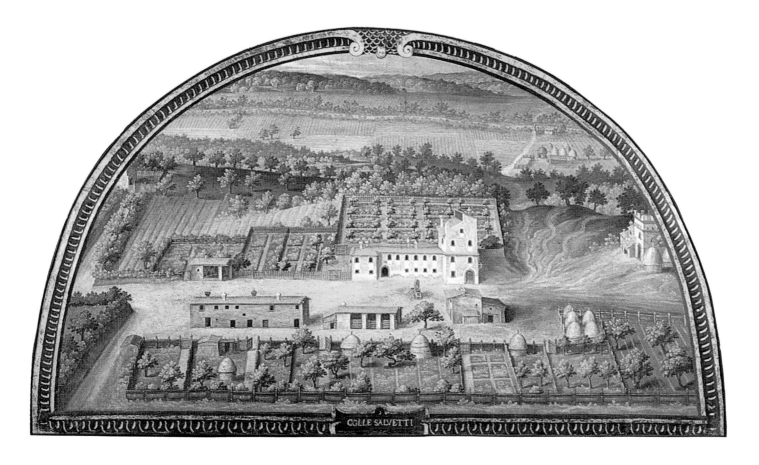

COLLE SALVETTI

intervention–the opening up of arcades and loggias above them at Villa La Suvera (added in 1507 by Pope Julius II)—is sufficient to demonstrate the very different mentality with which the relationship between building and countryside was viewed.

It is true, of course, that the loggia is not an unheard-of stylistic innovation but an ancient architectural legacy from the Mediterranean region, an internal/external space that expands the house (and farmhouse), a space that is both sheltered and ventilated, a filter between the interior and the natural world. Thus, we are not talking about a novelty but rather witnessing, in this Sienese example, the reappropriation of a native and updated tradition in a context that has finally liberated itself from the restraints of caution.

An interesting case of stylistic experimentation can be seen in Peruzzi's project for Belcaro (1533). The reconstruction of this villa-castle, as indicated by a drawing in the Uffizi, called for the creation of an external loggia, along the entire length of the

existing building, which to all intents and purposes constitutes a covered central road, erected on two floors and intended to join, on the opposite side, a courtyard and a "dining hall below and the drawing room and bedroom above." This idea obviously inspired the unusual evolution of the courtyard-cum-corridor of Villa Pannocchieschi d'Elci at Anqua, the residential suites being on one side and the servants' quarters and domestic offices directly opposite on the other.

In the territory around Lucca the villas Guinigi at Matraia and Buonvisi at San Pancrazio (both built near the end of the 16th century) are remarkable for the imposing size of the porticoes that pierce the rear façades and allow the buildings to participate in the ambient countryside, projecting their interiors out towards the wide panoramic landscapes beyond the gardens. In fact, the unusually large portico of Villa Buonvisi, which consists of five deep, wide bays, is high enough to contain and protect two rows of windows, one above the other.

The villa-farm of the Medici at Colle Salvetti, in a lunette fresco painted by Giusto Utens (Museo di Firenze com'era, Florence).

The circular chapel designed by Baldassarre Peruzzi for Villa Celsi at Celsa, Siena.

During the later years of the 16th century and throughout the 17th century the functions of the villa underwent progressive alteration in order to accommodate changes in the habits of a privileged social class increasingly inclined to devote its wealth and time to the luxury of the *villeggiatura* and in some cases (the Riccardi and Feroni families, for example) to open competition with no less than the Medici household and its inherited riches. Thus, Villa Feroni (Bellavista) at Buggiano can, in sheer size, bear comparison with not a few palaces in the city.

To trace the evolution of this phenomenon in the various territorial areas of Tuscany means being aware of a transformation that does not directly influence the architectural characteristics of the villa (these remain practically unaltered) but that does certainly reflect artistic tastes and stylistic fashions, those factors, that is, which are complementary to architecture.

Added to the pleasure of owning property in the country was now the pleasure of enjoying such a privilege in the most congenial manner, allowing for every possible recreational diversion.

This was the moment when the "productive" role of the villa as an agricultural center started to diminish. Instead, it came to be regarded more and more as the resort of cultured (and sometimes not so cultured) guests and as a stage for worldly entertainments. The concepts of *utilitas* made way for those of *divertissement* and aesthetics, in keeping with the new vogue for "villa living." Wealth and pleasure, those markers of the proprietor's economic standing, weakened the Albertian "virtue" of the villa, and meditative leisure suffered contamination from an increase in those noisy and often licentious pastimes that would now be deemed absolutely indispensable if the social standing of the country house was to receive its due. The holiday occupations of the leading families vied with those of the court, and they competed with one another in an effort to make the interiors of their villas as beautiful and up-to-date as possible. It is as if Alberti's advice about the decoration of the villa was now being put into practice: "all the allurements of elegance and pleasure are admissible."

The result of this gathering activity was to create an acute contrast between the impoverished architecture of the façade and the lavish decoration of the interiors.

The more enthusiastic the owner, the more the villa became the catalyst for a wealth of essential elements: the tree-lined avenue leading up to the main entrance, the ancestral chapel, the lemon-house, the pages' rooms, the servants' quarters, the fountain, the nymphaeum, and, obviously, the garden as the external continuation of the decorative splendor inside the villa. The creation of the garden, seen as a superfluous piece of architectural display, was one decidedly arrogant way of showing dissatisfaction with normality, even that of the natural world. Reflecting a culture that pursued new fashions and new myths, the garden had become a place ideally suited to outdoor life and play. It acted as a filter between the cares of the city and the isolated microcosm of the villa, while also serving as a screen to conceal the perhaps prosaic aspects of the cultivated land that surrounded it.

MEDICI
FAMILY

COAT OF ARMS
(before 1465):
Or seven balls gules, six in orle
and one at fess point

Opposite: The façade of Villa Medici at Careggi, with the addition of an avant-corps crowned by a deep, attic-level loggia. As for this feature, one should note the density of the colonnade, which no doubt represents a bold solution to a structural problem, a solution worthy of a great architect.

Below: The corner loggetta at Villa Medici at Careggi, with it's ceiling décor of grottesche, sham pergolas, comic scenes of country life, and allegories, all painted by Michelangiolo Cinganelli in 1618.

VILLA MEDICI AT CAREGGI
Florence

While justly celebrated (and perhaps also somewhat mythicized) as the site of the philosophical disputations of the Neoplatonist Academy founded by Marsilio Ficino and as the meeting place of artists and intellectuals attracted by the patronage of the Medici, this villa is of less interest from an architectural point of view.

Though it was frequented by Donatello, Leon Battista Alberti, Michelangelo, Pico della Mirandola, Poliziano, Cristoforo Landino, Filippo Valori, Carlo Marsuppini, and others, these luminaries were apparently satisfied with the building's predominantly medieval aspect. At all events, they did nothing to encourage the Medici patrons to seek architectural solutions more in keeping with the significance and prestige of such a brilliant and avant-garde coterie of Renaissance men.

As if from deep-rooted Florentine habit,

The interior courtyard at Villa Medici at Careggi, with its facing porticoes formed of round-headed arcades. This is surely one of the areas within the villa where the hand of Michelozzo can be felt.

the Medici took care to display caution, frugality, and traditional forms on the building's exterior, preferring to save their delight in artistic quality for the interior (Verrocchio's *Putto with Dolphin* and frescoes by Pontormo and Bronzino once

adorned the villa at Careggi).

It was probably Giovanni di Bicci, founder of the Medici family, who acquired in June 1417, for 800 gold florins, "a palazzo with courtyard, loggia, well, cellar, chapel, stable, dovecote, tower, and walled

garden" from a certain Tommaso Lippi. In 1459, in a letter to his father, Galeazzo Maria Sforza described the Careggi villa as a "beautiful palazzo," which, "in the way of rooms and kitchens and parlors and every manner of furnishing," lacked nothing in comparison with palaces in the city.

This suggests that by the time of the younger Sforza's Florentine visit the structure had already assumed its definitive shape, or very nearly so. According to Vasari, this was the work of Michelozzo

A detail of a room on the piano nobile in Villa Medici at Careggi. On the carved-wood plinth rests a marble copy of a portrait bust representing Cosimo the Elder.

Carved-stone mantelpiece, dating from 1465, in the salon on the piano nobile in Villa Medici at Careggi.

Michelozzi, commissioned by Cosimo de' Medici the Elder.

In recent years the corner *loggetta* with its little Ionic columns, which was added to the south front, has been attributed to Giuliano da Sangallo. Attribution aside, however, not even the *loggetta* (which attests to the need for enlarging and proportionally opening up the building) can alter–except as a separate and partial embellishment–the overall fortified character of the house. It is a structure essentially closed to the outside, scarped at the base, and protected on top by an

overhanging crenelated gallery supported on corbels, for the purpose of raining missiles down on would-be aggressors.

It was probably Michelozzo who covered the gallery with a roof to mask the crenellations, who designed the two facing arcades, resting on awkward Corinthian columns, in an attempt to regularize the trapezoid shape of the courtyard, and who added a carved stone mantelpiece to one of the rooms to lend it some character. Still, there are simply not enough such elements of camouflage and stylistic touches to impart a clearly Renaissance stamp to the exterior.

In 1492, Lorenzo the Magnificent died at Careggi. Then in 1527, upon the expulsion of the Medici from Florence, the villa was sacked and burned by the republican faction.

Restored by Alessandro (the first Duke of Florence) after 1532, it was later adorned, over the course of the 17th century, with grotesques and landscapes in the lunettes and vaults of the banquet hall on the ground floor, supposedly executed by painters from Michelangiolo Cinganelli's workshop. In 1779, by order of Grand Duke Pietro Leopoldo, the Office of the Royal Possessions transferred the villa (for 30,000 *scudi*) to Vincenzo di Donato Orsi, who in 1848 sold it to Francis Joseph Sloane. Sloane added the striking entrance to the garden (flanked by pilasters and twin structures in the Neoclassical style), modified the arrangement of the parterres of the garden itself, and constructed the *limonaia*, or lemon-house, with its crown of neo-Gothic battlements.

*A room on the ground floor,
in Villa Medici at Careggi,
with lunettes and vaults
featuring a décor of
grottesche and landscapes
attributed to the workshop
of Michelangiolo
Cinganelli.*

VILLA MEDICI AT POGGIO A CAIANO
Prato

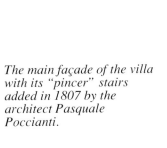

MEDICI
FAMILY

COAT OF ARMS
(after 1465):
Or six balls in orle, five gules
and one azure in chief, charged
with three fleurs-de-lis

The Florentine land registry of 1480 records that several years earlier, Lorenzo the Magnificent had acquired from Giovanni Rucellai "a ruined residence at Poggio a Caiano, called l'*anbra*." As Vasari tells it, Lorenzo intended to build a grandiose villa (the first of that basic type in Tuscany) over the previous structure, and in 1485 he "had a number of models made by Francione and others," including Giuliano da Sangallo. The latter "made his so different in form from the others, and so much in keeping with Lorenzo's fancy, that he began at once to execute it, as it was the best of all."

Lorenzo's villa, as it looks today, is the product of a number of modifications that have somewhat changed its original appearance. In 1575 the architect Alfonso Parigi raised the roof about a meter and a half and increased the overhang of the eaves; in the 1700s the clock gable was added; and in the 19th century the original rectilinear staircase was replaced by two semicircular flights designed by Pasquale Poccianti in 1807 and later executed by the architect Giuseppe Cacialli. These additions, however, need not be viewed as infelicitous or intrusive. The clock gable, for example, gives a vertical thrust to the façade, and the curving lines of the double stairs help to mitigate the lack of harmony between the massive body of the villa and the open arcade below, imparting an unquestionable majesty to the whole.

With regard to the original look of Lorenzo's country palace, it is worth considering a few of the formal aspects of Sangallo's design. Primary importance has always been given–and corroborated by comparisons with classical models–to the building's monumental basement (comparable, in the opinion of many scholars, to the *basis villae* of ancient

The main façade of the villa with its "pincer" stairs added in 1807 by the architect Pasquale Poccianti.

36

Roman prototypes) and the defining role played by the central, pedimented portico.

As for the *basis villae*, the references cited by various scholars might seem more legitimate if they took into account that in the Roman era, substructures and *cryptoportici* (arcaded basements), were often necessitated by sloping terrain, which is clearly not the case at Poggio a Caiano. Moreover, in ancient Roman villas the distribution of masses did not usually tend toward great height, and therefore the relationship between the supporting structure and the part supported was quite different from the one exhibited in Lorenzo de' Medici's country residence.

On the other hand, still keeping to Classical models, the unnatural height of the arcaded basement might be said to be derived from the example of a temple podium. Nor should we exclude the possibility that–as has been pointed out–the structure's elevation from the ground, rather than corresponding to an attitude of aristocratic "detachment," was actually dictated by the far more prosaic need to raise the villa in order to protect it (as they might have hoped at the time) from the malarial miasmas emanating from the marshes near the River Ombrone, which bordered the Medici property.

As for the Ionic portico and its pediment,

At Villa Medici at Poggio a Caiano, a steeply foreshortened view of the arcaded basement.

it must be pointed out (beyond the usual apologies for this Classical "quotation") that the pediment seems not to fit in with the rest of the façade design, since, contrary to the rules of composition, its apex rises above the sill line of the second order of windows. The gentle pitch of the eaves (which some say is reminiscent of the low, elongated roof-slope of Etruscan temples) suggests that the pediment's form was dictated by the width of the portico below, and by a desire not to have the surface of the triangular tympanum overlap the area of the two pre-existing central windows.

Other details lend color to the hypothesis that the pediment was added at some later date. The glazed terracotta frieze, for example, reminiscent of the Della Robbias but executed by Sansovino, has been attributed to the building phase under Pope Leo X (early 16th century). Moreover, the form of the Medici crest at the center of the tympanum, adorned with four undulating ribbons (and with no fleurs-de-lis on the balls), was widespread during the second decade of the 16th century.

It is also worth pointing out the fact, hitherto unrecorded, that the architrave of the portico ends beneath the cornice of the left-hand window (viewed from the front). This oddity suggests still other hypotheses: that the window itself might have been (inexplicably) shifted toward the middle of the façade some time after the construction of the portico; or that the presumed ideal perfectionism of Lorenzo's country palace was compromised in its realization by inaccurate workmanship on the part of masons in the employ of his descendants.

Upon Lorenzo's death in 1492, the villa's first floor above the arcaded basement was still not covered, and in all likelihood the work site remained inactive until 1512, when the Medici returned to

The salone of Leo X, Villa Medici at Poggio a Caiano. The polychrome stuccowork decorating the barrel vault was executed in 1519-21 by Andrea di Cosimo Feltrini. Note the "yoke," "laurel branch," and "rings with feathers," all emblems of the Medici.

43

Page 42: The salone of Leo X, Villa Medici at Poggio a Caiano. The lunette, with its pastoral scene from the pagan myth of Vertumnus and Pomona, was frescoed in 1520-25 by Jacopo Pontormo. On the upper walls below, the personifications of Piety, Virtue, and Justice came from the hand of Alessandro Allori, working in 1578-82.

Page 43: In the salone of Leo X, the Garden of the Hesperides above and allegories of Fame, Glory, and Honor below, all frescoed by Alessandro Allori.

The marble fireplace in the so-called apartment of Bianca Cappello on the ground floor.

Florence after their exile.

Between 1513 and 1521, Pope Leo X, son of Lorenzo the Magnificent, completed the construction of the central *salone,* installing the barrel vault and calling upon Pontormo, Andrea del Sarto, and Franciabigio to paint the walls of that great hall with frescoes illustrating the glories of the Medici dynasty–in the guise of mythological figures (Vertumnus and Pomona). Andrea del Sarto's *Triumph of Caesar* (1519-21), in accordance with the iconographical schema devised by Paolo Giovio, alludes to the gifts sent to Lorenzo by the Sultan of Egypt, while *The Return of Cicero,* by Franciabigio, commemorates the return of Cosimo the Elder, *pater patriae,* from exile. In Franciabigio's fresco the architectural structures–that is, the two

central-plan temples–present formal characteristics of a quality and complexity unknown to the Florentine architecture of the time, and are distinguished by a precocious Mannerism unlike that of Vasari, Ammannati, and Buontalenti.

The glazed terracotta frieze by Andrea Sansovino in the entablature of the Ionic portico, which illustrates the Platonic myth of the soul's path through the temporal dimension, is also believed to have been executed during the reign of Leo X.

The walls around the villa, added for defensive purposes, must also have been built before 1536. Emperor Charles V found them excessive when visiting Poggio a Caiano on the occasion of his daughter's marriage to Duke Alessandro de' Medici. The walls were reinforced around 1570 with corner bulwarks that bear the mark of Buontalenti.

There are also documents testifying that in 1545-46 the garden, the lawns surrounding the villa, and the court for pallacorda (an early form of tennis) were installed under the direction of Niccolò Pericoli, known as Il Tribolo.

From 1578 to 1582, the task of completing the fresco decoration of the salone of Leo X was entrusted to Alessandro Allori. Aside from working on–and adding to–the frescoes of Andrea del Sarto and Franciabigio, he also painted the missing "histories" and a few allegories. In *Titus Flaminius Speaking to the Achaeans and Scipio at Syphax's Banquet,* Allori placed events and characters in monumental colonnades giving onto landscapes with an archaeological flavor. His compositions are filled with "portraits" of exotic animals (leopards, lions, elephants) that were supposed to represent the opulence of a royal retinue in ancient times but were also symbolic of the

economic and social prestige attained by the Grand Dukes of Tuscany.

The most important new artistic addition of the 17th century was the fresco decoration of the "stucco room" (*on the piano nobile or first floor up*), an undertaking that Prince Ferdinando de' Medici entrusted to the painter Anton Domenico Gabbiani. The subject depicted is Florence presenting Cosimo the Elder to Jove (1698).

The theater on the ground floor and the roofing of the outer galleries connecting the facing rooms on the second floor date from the early Lorraine period (1772 and 1794, respectively). From the very beginning, these galleries, situated in the recessed area at the back of the edifice, were the weak points of the overall design and its greatest shortcoming. Because of the unfortunate central location of the double-story *salone*, which divided the upper floor of the building in two parts, the front apartments could only be reached by way of these open-air passages.

During the brief regency of Maria Louisa of Etruria (1802-07), the architect Poccianti designed the outer stairways and began the construction of the interior staircase that replaced Sangallo's original one. In the Napoleonic era, Princess Elisa Baciocchi hired Luigi Catani to paint the entrance hall with monochrome frescoes: *Angelo Poliziano Crowning the Bust of Homer and Giuliano da Sangallo Showing Lorenzo the Magnificent the Model of the Villa of Poggio a Caiano.*

Princess Elisa was also responsible for the transformation of other rooms into ornate "French-style baths" (executed by Giuseppe Cacialli). Likewise due to the House of Lorraine were the layout of the garden, the building of the lemon-house (from Poccianti's plans), and the

construction (from designs by Alessandro Manetti) of the little iron suspension bridge spanning the Ombrone (1833).

Turned into a royal residence for the House of Savoy in 1865, the villa was partially refurnished (under the direction of

Alessandro Allori, Allegories of Magnanimity, Majesty, and Generosity, a fresco in the salone *of Leo X at Villa Medici at Poggio a Caiano.*

At Villa Medici at Poggio a Caiano, a detail of Andrea del Sarto's Triumph of Caesar, a fresco in the salone of Leo X. Especially notable are the architectural setting and the exotic animals (a giraffe, a turkey, a monkey, a parrot, a salamander). The right part of the fresco was painted in 1581 by Alessandro Allori.

Antonio Sajler) and redecorated–witness the Billiard Room. The furniture and wall paintings of the rooms of King Victor Emmanuel II and his wife by morganatic marriage, the Countess of Mirafiori, typify the tastes of the period.

Alessandro Allori, *The Roman Consul Titus Flaminius Speaking to the Achaeans, a fresco in the* salone *of Leo X at Villa Medici at Poggio a Caiano. The story refers to the prescence of Lorenzo the Magnificent at a session of the Cremona Diet.*

49

Alessandro Allori, Scipio at the Banquet of Syphax, King of Numidia, a fresco of 1581 in the salone *of Leo X at Villa Medici at Poggio a Caiano. The painting allegorizes the state visit paid by Lorenzo the Magnificent to Naples in 1479, which ended with the signing of a peace treaty.*

The decorative program
carried out by Gaetano
Lodi, under commission
from King Victor Emmanuel
of Savoy, on the walls and
vaults of the Billiard Room
on the ground floor of Villa
Medici at Poggio a Caiano.

The Billiard Room at Villa
Medici in Poggio a Caiano,
with furnishings and
decorations dating from the
Savoy period. The lunettes
and the sham pergola on
the vault were painted by
Gaetano Lodi.

At Villa Medici in Poggio a Caiano, a detail of the decorative wallpaper in a room on the second floor, above the piano nobile. Dating from the time of Elisa Baciocchi, the paper, with its scenes involving American Indians, came from the firm of Desfossé.

MAGNIFICUS LAURENTIUS MEDICES

CAIANI EXEMPL AB SIBI A IULIANO SANGALLIO ARCHITECTO INSIGNI EXIBITUM LAUDAT ATQUE AD EIUS NORMAM NOBILE PRÆTORIUM EXCHARI IUBET

Luigi Catani, Giuliano da Sangallo Showing Lorenzo the Magnificent the Model of the Villa of Poggio a Caiano, a grisaille fresco in the entrance hall on the piano nobile.

VILLA LE VOLTE
Siena

This structure, which Sigismondo Chigi wanted built as a refuge where he might "escape his troubles," was designed by Baldassarre Peruzzi. It is considered a kind of "dress rehearsal" for the more famous villa that Peruzzi built in Rome for Agostino Chigi, Sigismondo's brother, which later came to be known as La Farnesina and which has been called the "most astonishing work of architecture of the early 16th century."

With these two edifices, thanks to Peruzzi's brilliance, the Chigi, a rich and powerful family of merchants and bankers who were enemies of the Medici, succeeded in surpassing their rivals, at least where villa architecture was concerned, inaugurating a clearly new and original typology. Le Volte was Peruzzi's first attempt at adapting to the concept of villa life a building plan in the form of two sections projecting perpendicularly from a central block (so as to create a kind of courtyard open on one side). This design was then formally perfected and stylistically refined in the Farnesina (1506-11).

Another distinguishing feature of Le Volte was the placement of two loggias, one above the other, on the side of the main block facing the half-courtyard (a solution earlier adopted by Rossellino for the rear façade of Palazzo Piccolomini at Pienza).

From the combination of these two typological characteristics, which both aim at opening up the structure to the outside, the Le Volte prototype was born, though the villa may in fact be a transformation of an earlier building. If so, this would explain the irregularities in the dimensions of the projecting wings.

That this villa constitutes a prototype (and a novelty in the Tuscan region) is proved by the fact that its outside walls were once "entirely painted" (a true rarity),

as Fabio Chigi wrote in his *Commentarii* around 1523. The polychromy of the façades had its natural complement in the frescoes adorning the many vaulted ceilings inside (from which the villa derives its name, which means "The Vaults"). These were painted from 1520 to 1523 by various

artists of Peruzzi's circle.

The importance of the villa's relationship to the outside is underscored by the stone bench that runs continuously along the perimeter of the building at its base–another peculiarity seldom found in Tuscan villas.

In 1605, a "restoration" brought some radical changes to the building: the upper loggia of the central façade was enclosed; a loggia on the other side was opened up; the window and door frames were renovated; and the previously painted outer walls were plastered.

This comprehensive view allows us to appreciate the special characteristics of Villa Le Volte's planes and volumes. It also reveals the differing widths of the projecting wings that, together with the central block, form the forecourt.

Villa Le Volte seen from a corner, an angle that brings out the curious off-center placement of the ashlar-framed entrance door, the end pilasters set short of the actual corner, and the continuous stone bench along the base, a feature that stresses the extreme horizontality of the building relative to its height.

DELLA ROVERE FAMILY

COAT OF ARMS:
Azure an uprooted oak or, with branches folded in a double St. Andrew's cross

Below: The villa set within the beautiful Sienese countryside.

Opposite: The three superposed loggias overlooking the valley.

VILLA LA SUVERA
Pievescola, Siena

In 1507 Pope Julius II (Giuliano Della Rovere) set about creating a villa from the old fortified palace given him by the Republic of Siena, situated on the western slopes of the Montagnola.

The existing edifice was restructured and enlarged by the addition of a building mass whose front and rear façades are characterized by three deep loggias, one on top of the other. Arranged asymmetrically with respect to each other (one at the far end of the rear façade, the other in a corner of the avant-corps of the original palace, at the front), the loggias give the structure a highly unusual formal appearance. Indeed, this peculiarity of having two three-storied openings, with arches supported by pilasters on the ground floor and by columns on the other two floors, is evidence of a wish to brighten and open up the mass of the building and to let the domestic life inside the villa partake of the sights of the surrounding countryside. The superimposed space of the triple arcades is a concrete expression of the desire to create, at each story, an extension of the inner space onto the landscape outside, an appropriately protected and decorated lookout in which to linger and enjoy the beautiful views.

This emphatic projection of domesticity into nature, suggested by the large and numerous loggias (whose insistent repetition in the context of a single building is clearly unprecedented in Tuscany), appears to reflect the enlightened character of Julius II, a strong-willed, elitist patron of the arts who commissioned architectural and artistic works by such major Renaissance figures as Bramante (the Belvedere complex, the loggias in the courtyard of San Damaso, the plans for Saint Peter's Basilica in the Vatican), Raphael (the frescoes for the Stanze della Segnatura), and Michelangelo (the funerary monument for Julius himself and the Sistine Chapel frescoes).

The elegant formal treatment of some of the architectural elements (the Tuscan and Ionic capitals of the loggia columns, the balustrades of the front arcade) and decorative motifs (the painted *grotescues* on the vaults of a loggia on the *piano nobile*) are further confirmations of a refinement that was guided by a demanding patron.

Even the entrance to the villa, situated obliquely with respect to the façade, seems deliberately calculated. Greatly enhancing the perspective and setting, it frames the angle created by the juxtaposition of the 16th-century façade, pierced by the loggia

Page 66: At Villa La Suvera, a detail of the portico giving access to the ground floor on the side facing the valley.

Page 67: The deep arcaded and vaulted galleries on the façade of Villa La Suvera facing the mountains.

Opposite: At Villa La Suvera, a corner of the salotto, *furnished in a refined antiquarian manner.*

arcades, with the solid, scarped avant-corps of the old palace.

After the death of Julius II, the Della Rovere family sold the pontiff's villa to Niccola and Sigismondo Chigi, in 1534.

The arrangement of the garden, while keeping in part to earlier designs and making use of old garden ornaments, shows signs of recent modifications.

Below: The most striking characteristic of the salone arises from the fine-tuned relationship between the formal and stylistic qualities of the fireplace and the flanking pair of doors.

The chapel, the 19th-century lamps, and the gazebo-like aviary make an eclectic ensemble on the piazzale they share with the Villa La Suvera.

A few of the ornamental fragments that abound in the garden at Villa La Suvera.

VILLA DI VICOBELLO
Siena

CHIGI
FAMILY

*Right: The villa seen from
one of the garden terraces.
In the foreground, at the
center of a flower bed, a
topiary version of the
Chigi's six armorial
mountains bordered by a
low box hedge.*

*Below: To the left of the
residence, the chapel
incorporated in the one-
story service quarters.*

Rising at the top of a series of terraces,
this 16th-century construction, built by the
Chigi family, is distinguished by its
concentration of windows at the center of
the façade, which looks onto Siena.

This same middle section is marked by
three arch moldings and by pilasters in low
relief dividing and framing the window
areas. The double stringcourse between the
ground floor and the main floor and the strip
demarcating the attic have led some to
attribute the villa's design to Baldassarre
Peruzzi. These formal details, however, are
not enough to confirm such a hypothesis.

The space between the main block of the
villa and the service buildings is shaped like
an open courtyard, from which the terraces
lead downward in a series of gardens.

In the salone *at Villa di Vicobello, the trompe-l'oeil curtains painted by the decorator Spampani are pulled back to reveal deep views of pleasant landscapes.*

Opposite: At Villa di Vicobello, an exedra-like structure styled in the manner of Peruzzi serves as a focal point at the end of the lemon garden.

Right: This arch, crowned by the six emblematic mountains of the Chigi, comes at the end of a long tree-lined avenue and opens into Villa di Vicobello.

78

CELSI
FAMILY

COAT OF ARMS:
Gules a lion rampant argent, a
bend vert

ALDOBRANDINI
FAMILY

COAT OF ARMS:
Azure a bend or double
embattled, flanked by six
eight-pointed stars

*Overall view of the villa
beyond the foreground
garden all'italiana planted
by the Aldobrandini at the
turn of the 20th century.
At the right stands the
cylindrical chapel
attributed to Peruzzi.*

VILLA CELSI
Celsa, Siena

In all likelihood this medieval castle–formerly the property of the Celsi family and now belonging to the Aldobrandini–was first transformed into a villa on the initiative of Mino Celsi, a man of letters and member of the Accademia degli Intronati.

The signs of the 16th-century renovation. attributed to Baldassarre Peruzzi, are to be found above all in the retaining walls of the terraces, the layout of the front garden, the circular-plan chapel, and the low dividing wall in front–with three portals–that turns the triangular space between the two symmetrical and turreted wings of the castle into an interior courtyard.

In other words, the Cinquecento alterations, apparently no more than a cosmetic embellishment, actually succeeded in harmonizing the existing convergence of the two opposing structures and giving it the stage-like quality of a backdrop, combining the old complex with the new annexes in a unified spatial whole that is decidedly more stately and "modern."

The quest for theatrical effects is visible in the descending terraces, which are linked by a series of ramps, stairways, and walks adorned with pairs of pilasters marking the successive openings in the retaining walls. The axes of these walks have, as their poles of interest, a semicircular basin (at the center of a little square commanding a fine view), and a fish pond surrounded by a high, balustraded parapet adorned with "rustic" encrustations and allegorical statues. The long, telescopic perspectives running between these poles and the other formal fulcrum that is the chapel are dotted with vases and small obelisks and flanked by undulating, ball-topped topiary hedges that define and accompany the paths to follow.

The most priceless architectural feature of this decorative ensemble, though not in

Opposite: Situated on a hilltop overlooking the Rosia Valley, the Villa Celsi–an ancient castle–boasts two battlemented towers connected by a low 15th-century wall that both gives access to and encloses the interior courtyard.

harmony with the surroundings (of which the neo-Gothic renovation of the castle is part), is the chapel, attributed to Peruzzi. With its diminutive cylindrical shape, characterized by pilaster strips, niches, and oculi, and crowned by a small conical cupola, the chapel now stands like an event unto itself.

At Villa Celsi, the path leading to the fish pond, the hedges on either side clipped in the form of undulating parapets.

At Villa Celsi, a view upon the sequence of pilasters paired left and right on axis with a semicircular and balustraded basin-fountain. Of special interest is the way the formal and stylistic character of the architectural elements, originally plaster-coated, harmonize with the ornamental vases and volutes cut from stone.

VILLA DI BELCARO
Siena

TURAMINI
FAMILY

COAT OF ARMS:
Party undé, or and azure, a
rising crescent moon azure in
the first and a six-pointed star
or in the second, both in chief

A drawing by Baldassarre Peruzzi at the Uffizi represents the plans for a structure to be built within the walls of the castle of Belcaro, alongside an existing "palazzo." The design shows two orders of loggias opening onto a central space surrounded by still another arcade that is flanked by a "dining hall, reception room, and chamber," as well as service rooms: a wine-cellar on the ground floor and an apartment above "for the caretaker." The plan also shows, in the little courtyard adjacent to the castle entrance, a loggia with "bedroom and study" above it, as well as "a garden" and a "secret garden" in the remaining terrain to the right of the palazzo, marked off by a new dividing wall.

All these notations on the plan indicate that the architect intended to keep the boundary wall around the castle intact (while turning the parapet into a panoramic walkway) and to concentrate the life and activities of the new villa complex within the medieval enclosure. The transformation of the castle into a villa was undertaken by the banker Crescenzio Turamini, who had acquired the Belcaro property for this purpose in 1525.

Today, all that remains of Peruzzi's reconstruction plan is the rather original idea of the courtyard-passage between the two facing buildings, which is screened off from the garden by a wall now pierced by two openings. In fact, neither the external formal elements of the villa (which are somewhat lacking in character and were, moreover, restored in the 19th century by Serafino Billi) nor the service quarters opposite (rebuilt in 1865 by Giuseppe Partini) give any indication that Peruzzi might have been involved in their construction On the other hand, the wall of the entrance to the present-day garden (with its two portals and central niche housing the well), the little church of Saints James and Christopher, and the adjacent, frescoed loggia, originally part of the secret garden, can be traced to the work executed between 1533 and 1535.

Other signs of Peruzzi's influence can be

Opposite: A detail of the villa's façade and the sentry path along the top of the medieval wall that encloses the Belcaro complex.

Below: A view of the villa and the garden behind it. At the far corner of the house, above a window, note the little balcony that connects the building with the sentry path along the top of the medieval wall.

At Villa di Belcaro, the loggia of the secret garden. The paintings on the lunette and the vaults, representing rustic and mythological subjects, were executed by Giorgio di Giovanni around 1535.

found in the decorative motifs of the loggia (which include rustic scenes, arbors, and mythological subjects) and in *The Judgment* *of Paris* fresco on the vault of the villa's entrance hall.

Page 90: A detail of the travertine framework around the well at Villa di Belcaro.

Page 91: The present garden with the chapel and the triple arcade of the secret garden dating from the 15th century. Above the wall rise a pair of neomedieval towers.

The courtyard at Villa di Belcaro, paved with stone laid herring-bone fashion, takes the form of a wide corridor running between the main residence and the service quarters opposite. At the end stands the enclosure wall with two archways, on either side of a well, giving access to the little garden.

VILLA NICCOLINI
Camugliano, Pisa

NICCOLINI
FAMILY

COAT OF ARMS:
Azure a lionized leopard argent rampant, a bend gules; with chief azure, charged with quadruple-dovetailed label gules surmounting a pontifical tiara or with infulae and papal keys in a St. Andrew's cross in same, flanked by two fleurs-de-lis

Opposite: This view dramatizes the massive towers projected from the corners of the villa.

Below: At the end of a tree-lined avenue rises the villa framed by the pillars of the entrance gate.

The original construction of this villa as a stronghold straddling the valleys of the Era and Cascina rivers was begun at the instigation of Duke Alessandro de' Medici. The four-towered structure, endowed with a drill-ground bordered by two symmetrical buildings that originally functioned as barracks and stables, was probably completed at the time of Cosimo I and converted for use as a villa.

Passing into the hands of the Gondi family, the land and buildings were subsequently purchased by Matteo di Giovanbattista Botti, who donated them to Grand Duke Cosimo II de' Medici in 1620. Cosimo II's successor, in a deed dated

The mighty sculptural group Hercules Slaying the Hydra, carved by Giovanni Bandini, called Giovanni dell'Opera, stands before Villa Niccolini like a cautionary presence.

September 23, 1637, then transferred the property to Senator Filippo Niccolini, who by a decree dated October 23, 1637, was given "the title of Marquess of Ponsacco and Camugliano."

The long avenue of *cypresses* leading up to the villa beautifully frames the structure's imposing mass. This dramatic effect grows in intensity until, inside the entrance gate, the perspective opens up into the sweeping front yard (the former drill-ground), a large lawn centered around the impressive 16th-century marble statue *Hercules Slaying the Hydra,* by Giovanni Bandini.

The 18th-century double staircase with balustrade, connecting the great lawn with a triple-arched loggia (now enclosed) on the main floor and the lookout loggias on the top floors of the south towers, lessens the building's fortified aspect, at least on the main façade. This military character, however, evident in the escarpments and the stone corner reinforcements at the base of the four towers, remains almost intact on the other façades. In all likelihood the particular typology adopted at Camugliano (with towers at the four corners) served as a model for the later Medici residence of L'Ambrogiana.

The Niccolini family were responsible for laying out the grounds in the English style, the low semicircular hedge (crowned by marble busts) surrounding the great lawn, and the garden to the side of the villa, loosely organized around the centerpiece of a circular pool with fountain. Inside the villa, the only notable architectural elements are the gray stone framing the doorways, the living-room fireplace, and the odd quatrefoil oculi of the entrance gallery. Then amidst all this austerity, the Romantic whimsy of the late 18th century suddenly appears in a room whose walls are painted with landscapes glimpsed through the delicate screen of a trompe-l'oeil neo-Gothic arcade.

The main façade of Villa Niccolini is remarkable for the well-integrated relationship among its vertical and horizontal parts.

VILLA I COLLAZZI
Giogoli, Florence

DINI
FAMILY

If the traditional though unlikely attribution of this villa to Michelangelo Buonarroti is to be believed, it must still be granted that the great Florentine kept very close–adding little of his own–to an architectural design already successfully implemented by Baldassarre Peruzzi in the villa of Le Volte at Siena and in the Roman Farnesina.

The documents far more modestly show that an existing manor (belonging in the 15th century to the Bonaventuri family) was transformed into a villa in 1534 by its owners at the time, Baccio and Agostino Dini. Another theory, that this construction was designed by the painter-architect Santi di Tito, is also highly suspect because Santi was a mere infant when the Dini were building their new house.

Quite apart from these more or less grandiose attributions, there can be no doubt that Villa I Collazzi represents one of the most accomplished and important examples of the vast repertory of Tuscan villas.

The south façade is adorned with a semicircular staircase and two small loggias on the top floor; the rear prospect boasts two raised loggias extending into both of the lateral wings. Such features as these, as well as the ashlar quoins highlighting the corners of the building and the importance of the arrangement of window frames and arches, give the structure its distinctive character and elegant majesty, despite the fact that it must be attributed to the episodic efforts of two amateur architects, perhaps aided by a particularly brilliant master builder.

A well-known engraving of the villa, by Giuseppe Zocchi (printed in 1744), gives an advance glimpse of the double entrance stairway from the open courtyard. This was added ten years later, in 1754, by Medea

The "open" courtyard contained within the villa's three wings, distinguished by their two tiers of arcaded loggias.

The south front of Villa I Collazzi completed in 1933 with the construction of one of the two small belvedere loggias.

Castelli, wife of a Dini, who also had the chapel painted in fresco by Giuseppe Meucci.

Left unfinished in the wing to the left of the courtyard, the villa was finally completed and rendered perfectly symmetrical in the 1930s by a "scholarly" operation commissioned by the Marchi family, current owners of the property.

The hilly countryside seen
from the forecourt of Villa
I Collazzi.

99

VILLA MEDICI AT CASTELLO
Florence

In 1477, Lorenzo and Giovanni di Pierfrancesco de' Medici came into possession of a "palace with battlements" located at "Olmo a Chastello" and formerly belonging to the Della Stufa family. After being enlarged by order of Giovanni, the "palace" was bequeathed to his wife, Caterina Sforza, and later to his son, Giovanni dalle Bande Nere, who had spent his childhood at Castello.

Elected Duke of Florence in 1537, Cosimo I, who had spent time at the family "palace," had it transformed into a villa, "so as to be able to live there comfortably with the court." He put Niccolò Pericoli, known as Il Tribolo, in charge of constructing the villa and designing the garden.

In Tribolo's general plan (conceptually accompanied by an iconological program drawn up by Benedetto Varchi), the villa took on the almost accidental role of a partition wall, a traversable "interruption" of a continuum of greenery and water that began with the long, tree-lined entrance avenue, went on into the garden across the

Right: The long main front facing the piazzale formerly overlooked a pair of fish ponds, which were filled in during the Lorraine period.

Below: An aerial view of the villa and its garden, the latter redesigned at the end of the 18th century.

Overleaf: A view of the garden. On the right is Tribolo's great fountain, which has now lost its bronze sculptural group of Hercules and Antaeus modeled by Bartolomeo Ammannati in 1560.

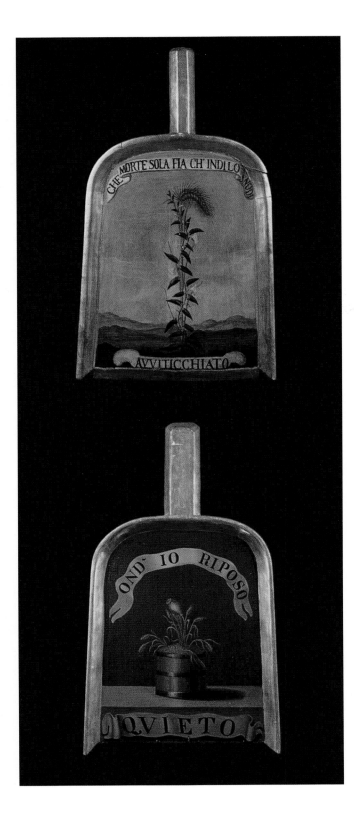

central Labyrinth of Venus, ran through the grotto, and ended at the upper pool surrounded by "wilderness."

All that remains of this ambitious plan, which symbolized, among other things, the territorial features of Cosimo's domain (the river, the wood, etc.), are the *fontana maggiore* ("great fountain") and the grotto.

Designed by Tribolo and built around 1546, the fountain–once the site of Bartolomeo Ammannati's sculpture group of Hercules crushing Antaeus (an allusion to Cosimo's defeat of his enemies)–was ideally supposed to collect the converging waters of other fountains arranged along the slope of the garden and to feed the descending water-chutes designed to parallel the avenue leading up to the villa. The grotto, cut into the embankment supporting the great pool of *The Appenine*, was meant to be a hidden place where the Mannerist delight in ambiguous imitations of nature could express itself in artificial stalactites, unpredictable ornamental waterworks, seashell mosaics, and stone animals shooting water "some from the beak, some from the wings, some from the claws, some from the ears, some from the nose."

It was only with Buontalenti that the villa assumed its definitive form. His design doubled the existing building mass and added the rusticated portal to the façade.

In the 17th century the villa, which was the favorite residence of Cardinal Giovanni Carlo de' Medici, was embellished with frescoes of Vigilance and Sleep, painted by Volterrano on the ceiling of the "Guard Room."

Since 1974, the villa has been the seat of the Accademia della Crusca.

VILLA MARTELLI
Gricigliano, Florence

MARTELLI
FAMILY

COAT OF ARMS:
Gules a griffin rampant

In 1478, for 100 florins, Niccolò d'Ugolino Martelli secured the lease "in perpetuity" of a small fortress and three farms from the Captains of Orsanmichele. The property had previously belonged to the Guadagni family, and had passed to the Captains during the 15th century. It was Martelli, therefore, who transformed the old structure, originally surrounded by a wall and moats, into a villa.

Starting in the early 16th century, the building began gradually to assume the appearance of an impressive villa and country seat surrounded by an unusual system of fish ponds (which replaced the moats) and a number of farmhouses. Important additions were made in the 17th century: the nymphaeum, the arch with stalactites, the wall fountain with rustic mosaics, and the carving in high relief of a

General view of the villa set within its lushly verdant landscape.

pelican feeding her young. These were followed in the 18th century by the chapel of Saint Joseph and the grotto decorated with encrustations, *spugne* (sponge-like stones), and fragments of colored ceramics and porcelain.

The uniqueness of this villa lies in its relationship to the surroundings. Its three austere façades, for example, are counterbalanced by the cheerful series of pools at different levels (interconnected by overflows or small locks), which lap against the base of the great building like a continuous canal. At the rear, a double-naved arcade leads into the central courtyard.

The walk that runs parallel to the sides of the ponds–equipped with seat-shaped parapets crowned by stone balls–allows a series of different framings to the local

109

The pools of water at different levels are among the most distinctive features of the Villa Martelli complex.

views that offer themselves to the passing gaze.

A perfect example of this is provided by the continuum that starts from the spatial division of the arcade, traverses the paved walkways, the bridge spanning the pools, and the gate with its two vase-topped pilasters, to arrive finally at the arched entrance to the grotto, surmounted by a gable bearing the face of a clock. Elsewhere, the villa's walls and the

Right: Martelli Coat of Arms, owners of Villa Martelli for five centuries.

low retaining walls of the ponds serve as signposts that direct the eye toward the broader panoramas of the distant hills.

These unusual spaces, unexpected ramifications, and traversable partitions are the very things that harmonize the villa's mass with its outbuildings and with the natural world (the water in the pools, the greenery, the landscape).

The rooms inside the villa tend to gravitate toward the "heart"–the central courtyard. Among the surprises within, there is a little theater with a balcony surviving from the 17th century, as well as rooms adorned with somewhat gaudy wall decorations. Particularly memorable among

The fish ponds, once the moat, mediate between the villa itself and its grounds. On the left is the arch and niche of the 17th-century nymphaeum.

the latter is the room with large landscapes painted between faux pilaster strips ending in monochrome atlantes, with doorjambs crowned by winged sphinxes alongside ovals depicting other country properties of the Martelli family.

The small, elegantly decorated theater evokes pleasant memories of times past at Villa Martelli.

VILLA MEDICI LA PETRAIA
Castello, Florence

MEDICI
FAMILY

COAT OF ARMS
(after 1469,
with grand-ducal crown):
Or six balls in orle, five gules
and one azure in chief, charged
with three fleurs-de-lis

*Right: A panoramic aerial
view of the villa and its
geometrically patterned
gardens, the latter laid out
in the 19th century. The
hillside park in the
background was created by
the Bohemian landscape
architect Joseph Frietsch.*

*Below: The villa seen from
a terrace midway between
the house above and the
gardens below.*

A fortified country house on this site, belonging to the Brunelleschi family in the 1300s, was acquired by Palla Strozzi in 1422 and then by Benedetto Salutati in 1468. After it had passed into Medici hands in 1530, Cosimo I made a present of the property to his son, Cardinal Ferdinando de' Medici (later Grand Duke), who turned it into a villa (in 1566, La Petraia was still referred to as a *casa da signore*).

According to the 17th-century art historian Filippo Baldinucci, it was Bernardo Buontalenti who was commissioned to transform the house. Yet given the lack of any authoritative documentation and the presence of a number of forgettable architectural and formal details, it is quite likely that the villa was the work of rather more modest master

Right: The courtyard was covered by a vast skylight during the residence of Victor Emmanuel of Savoy. The frescoes inside the arcade were painted by Il Volterrano (Baldassarre Franceschini), and those on the main walls by Cosimo Daddi.

Below: A wall in the courtyard with the Medici arms over the arched doorway.

Pages 118-119: In the glass-roofed inner courtyard at Villa Medici La Petraia, the arcade serves as a screen of columns through which to view walls frescoed by Cosimo Daddi with Scenes of Godfrey of Bouillon at the Siege of Jerusalem.

Below: Il Volterrano also painted The Triumphal Entry of Cosimo I into Siena, a scene that unfolds on the long wall of the arcade. Note the sham stairs with metal handrails at the base of the composition. In the painting above the real door, Catherine de' Medici, Queen-Regent of France, reigns at the center of the family into which she married, the Valois.

Opposite: On the far wall at the end of the arcade at Villa Medici La Petraia is a fresco by Baldassarre Franceschini, called Il Volterrano, representing Pope Leo X receiving King François I of France.

builders, such as Raffaello Pagni and Gherardo Mechini, who were in charge of overseeing operations until 1591. By that date the restructuring of the villa–which included a new arcade in the courtyard (with a loggia on top), symmetrical to the earlier one–had produced a square-plan, two-storied building dominated by the massive medieval tower, its overhanging crown pierced by arched windows. Also important during this phase was the realization of the garden on three terraced levels.

Christine of Lorraine (wife of Ferdinando I) was responsible for initiating, around 1589, the decoration of two façades of the inner courtyard with *Scenes of Godfrey of Bouillon at the Siege of Jerusalem,* painted by Cosimo Daddi. Later, in 1636, Prince Don Lorenzo de' Medici commissioned Baldassarre Franceschini, known as Il Volterrano, to paint the walls inside the courtyard arcades with the *Glories of the House of Medici.*

The construction of a small chapel on the ground floor dates from 1682; it was decorated in 1687 by the painter Carlo Mulinari. Around 1774, during the Lorraine period, this chapel was connected to the adjoining room (probably Cosimo III's bedroom)–which boasts a large fresco cycle of the *Glory of the Trinity and of All the Saints* (1696) on the walls and vault, by Rinaldo Botti and Pietro Dandini respectively–to form the present chapel of Ognissanti, or All Saints. In 1784, still in the Lorraine period, Grand Duke Pietro Leopoldo had Giambologna's *Fontana della Fiorenza,* a bronze Venus given that name in honor of the city of Florence, moved from the villa at Castello to La Petraia. This statue, "symbolizing Florence . . . who by wringing her hair made water shoot forth," was placed at the center of the Italian-style

garden to the east, on a marble base and shaft carved respectively by Tribolo and Pierino da Vinci.

In 1859 the villa passed to the royal House of Savoy and was restored and refurnished by Victor Emmanuel II, who turned the central courtyard into a ballroom, covering it with a skylight of glass and iron.

VILLA PANNOCCHIESCHI D'ELCI
Anqua, Siena

*Opposite: A room fashioned
from the central loggia at
the back the villa. The
vaults have been decorated
with grottesche in the
manner of Peruzzi.*

As indicated in the inscription under the family crest on the façade, this villa was built in 1572 by order of Count Marcello di Tommaso Pannocchieschi d'Elci. Little by little the modest farming community of Anqua grew up around it, establishing as its center the *piazzetta* formed by the small church, the boundary wall of the villa's courtyard, and the mass of the building itself.

As was the case at Belcaro, here too the plan of the villa complex (which rises up on a hill at the intersection of two valleys) is determined by two facing buildings, the residence and the service quarters. Both give on to a courtyard enclosed on its other two sides by dividing walls (the one separating it from the *piazzetta*, the other from the garden of the villa).

The similarity of this layout to Belcaro has led some to believe that it was the work of Peruzzi, overlooking the fact that the Sienese architect died in 1536. Moreover, even a cursory stylistic analysis of the formal details employed outside and inside

Below: Even the simple appointments of a hallway in Villa Pannocchieschi d'Elci bear the stamp of genuine aristocratic reserve.

Right: In the kitchen are preserved the fittings and arrangements of older times.

the residential building must decidedly preclude any attribution to Peruzzi.

Yet even without such an authoritative architectural pedigree, this villa, with its rear arcade and loggia, its brick façade, and the simple white window frames contrasting with the radiating ashlarwork of the portal, presents an overall stateliness of composition and a discreet sense of hierarchy in its relation to the service building opposite, which was restored in 1930. Especially charming is the courtyard-corridor, whose friendly dimensions are enhanced by the chromatic continuity of the building materials.

At Villa Pannocchieschi d'Elci, the courtyard-corridor with its central well dating from 1789. The rather odd merlons atop the enclosure wall at the far end are crowned with travertine spheres.

VILLA DI PRATOLINO
Florence

*This view of the park,
painted by Utens on the
surface of a lunette, does
not include the northern
section. Thus, it lacks both
the Appenine, a colossal
figure sculpture, and the
chapel.*

Of the many and much-heralded marvels of Pratolino, all that remains today (and perhaps not by accident) is Giambologna's gigantic, pensive statue *The Appenine*, by its sheer mass symbol and evidence of the former greatness and unsettling charm of what was once the most famous of the Medici villas. Built by Grand Duke Francesco I between 1570 and 1575, the villa reflected the solitary disposition and parascientific inclinations of its patron. His predilections were not so visible in its architectural aspects, however, as in its rich store of grottoes and automatons, its water organs that played marvelous music, its ascending and descending waterworks animating the great garden that fanned out from the north-south axis of the sloping terrain, at the extremities of which were the fountain of Jove (at the top) and the pool of the Washerwoman (at the bottom). The so-called "fountain promenade" was the directrix along which the park was divided into its separate events: the fountains of Perseus, Narcissus, Juno, and Parnassus, the Peasant's Fountain, and the fountains of the Ball-court and of the Frog.

Other "fine and stupendous inventions" connected to the water system were the grottoes of the Flood, the Weasel, the Frogs,

PRATOLINO

the Sponge, Galatea, Europa and Triton, the Samaritan Woman, the She-Bear, Cupid, Fame, and Pan. And the belly of *The Appenine* (built in 1579-80) actually contained two grottoes on top of each other where Francesco I might idle in introverted seclusion.

Near Giambologna's "giant," Buontalenti built a hexagonal chapel surrounded by a graceful arcade (intended for the servants, who attended the religious rites from outside), and crowned by an excessively high and disproportionately large dome.

In 1697 Prince Ferdinando (first-born son of Cosimo III) had a theater built on the third floor of the villa, from a design by Agostino Ferri. He also commissioned Giovan Battista Foggini to add a "flying stone dragon" behind Giambologna's colossus.

Yet the Pratolino estate was too personalized, too closely suited to the character of its first patron to satisfy the tastes, pleasures, and inclinations of his successors. During the Lorraine period, the villa and park were actually considered a superfluous luxury; thus, the farm buildings were rented to private interests and the remarkable complex was gradually

The onetime quarters for pages in service to the Medici at the villa subsequently owned by the Demidoff princes. The building is painted a 19th-century pink.

The Montili hunting lodge built at Villa di Pratolino in 1820 from plans drawn up by the architect Luigi Cambray Digny.

At the top of a short flight of steps stands the chapel enveloped in lush vegetation. It was erected at Villa di Pratolino in 1580 from a design prepared by Bernardo Buontalenti.

dismantled. In 1773 a number of statues were transferred to the Boboli Gardens, and in 1779 the villa was despoiled of its most prized furnishings. The pragmatic Pietro Leopoldo, insensitive to Pratolino's charm, had unambiguously decided that no "useless and unnecessary works of pure luxury" should be seen or made.

His son Ferdinando III was equally austere in his approach. In 1818, to limit maintenance expenses, he hired the Bohemian Joseph Frietsch to convert the garden to "the English style." And although Ferdinando III had the Montili hunting lodge built in 1820 from a design by Luigi Cambray Digny (an apparent sign of renewed interest in Pratolino), at the same time that he ordered the demolition (begun in 1821) of the villa, which by then was collapsing from neglect.

When Prince Paul Demidoff acquired Pratolino in 1872, it once again saw better days, however briefly. The Demidoffs turned the former Medici service quarters into a residence, adding on a new wing (used as a banquet hall) designed by Enrico Caramelli and Luigi Fusi. Then *the Appenine* was restored (in 1877); a copy of Jove, Bandinelli's original statue, was returned to its spot, the fountain of the same name; the cow-milker statue was restored to a rustic niche; the Fishpool of the Mask was also restored; and the foundation of the great aviary dismantled in 1788 was turned into a swimming pool.

VILLA MEDICI AT ARTIMINO
Prato

MEDICI
FAMILY

COAT OF ARMS
(after 1569,
with grand-ducal crown):
Or six balls in orle, five gules
and one azure in chief, charged
with three fleurs-de-lis

The hilly countryside around Artimino seen from the villa's meadow.

Built between 1594 and 1600 from plans by Bernardo Buontalenti, this villa is also called La Ferdinanda, because it was built by order of Grand Duke Ferdinando I de' Medici. Under the direction of master builders Santi Maiani and Gherardo Mechini, construction began in 1594 with the digging of the foundations. On December 16, 1596, the first stone was laid for what was to be a late version of a villa-fortress, with four distinctive, scarped bastions at the four corners of the edifice.

Since the villa was originally conceived as an occasional hunting lodge at the center of a vast "park" to satisfy the Grand Duke's passion for the chase, Buontalenti, by then an old man, thought it best not to bother with whimsical ornamentations, which would have been superfluous. As a result,

A detailed view of the outdoor stairs at Villa at Medici at Artimino. Built in 1930 from plans by the architect Lusini, these elaborate and decorative flights replaced the original and much simpler set of steps. The new project was commissioned by Countess Maraini Sommaruga.

Opposite: At Villa Medici at Artimino, a detail of the modern exterior stairs, their form inspired by ideas found in a sketch attributed to Buontalenti.

A side view of the east front of Villa Medici at Artimino where the entrance portal is surmounted by three windows giving onto a small balcony. The bastion on the near corner was broken at the level of the stringcourse and then transformed into a terrace.

the only outstanding formal features are the architraved loggia with five bays at the center of the west façade (originally connected to the ground via a rectilinear staircase) and the three great windows on the rear façade, which give onto a balcony.

The symmetrical design of the building plan is very simple: an atrium leads into corresponding *saloni* on either side of it, and each of these two great rooms communicates directly with a series of rooms running along its length. One of these saloni was the public hall, called the "salon of the villas" because its lunettes were adorned with frescoes by Giusto Utens depicting the various Medici estates. Some

Page 142: At Villa Medici at Artimino, the "Paradise" loggia with its barrel vault frescoed in 1599 by Domenico Cresti, called Il Passignano.

Page 143: The small interior chapel decorated by Il Passignano. The Resurrection of Lazarus above the altar is attributed to Giuseppe Niccolò Nasini.

Opposite: A pair of tondi representing personifications of Immortality and Public Happiness, painted by Domenico Cresti Il Passignano on the vault over the reception hall at Villa Medici at Artimino.

Below: The Banquet of Octavius and Livia, a fresco executed at the center of the vault over the reception hall, or salone pubblico, at Villa Medici at Artimino.

OTTAVIO

LIVIA

degree of architectural fantasy did, however, figure in the design of the many different forms of chimneys sprouting up from the roof.

Buontalenti's austere architecture, unalleviated even by surrounding gardens because of the lack of water on the west Artimino hill, was much later enhanced (in 1930) by the addition to the west front of a dramatic, projecting stairway with three flights, two of them curved. The work of the architect Enrico Lusini, these stairs were based on a design attributed to Buontalenti.

This architecturally simple villa does, however, hold some surprises inside, with its elaborate and remarkable series of fresco decorations. Starting with the so-called "Paradise Loggia," the subjects painted (by Domenico Passignano) keep primarily to a repertory of allegorical representations.

Thus on the loggia's vault we find images of History, Poetry, Solicitude, Diligence, Effort, and Patience, while on the ceiling of the great reception hall the *tondi* of *Public Happiness* and *Immortality* accompany *The Banquet of Octavian and Livia,* a revisitation of history celebrating the august grand-ducal couple. The small chapel is decorated with religious subjects, but after this exception the allegorical themes resume with the images of Heroic Virtue in what used to be Ferdinando's rooms and with the representations of Obedience, Chastity, and Fidelity presiding over the rooms of the Grand Duchess. Her apartment also includes the highly decorated *Ricetto del Poggiolo* ("Balcony Refuge"), which is covered with delightful grotesques attributed to Bernardino Poccetti.

At Villa Medici at Artimino, a corner of the kitchen with its great hearth set off by a simple framework of stone.

CAPPONI
FAMILY

COAT OF ARMS:
Party per bend sable and argent

VILLA
LA GAMBERAIA
Settignano, Florence

In 1610, Zanobi di Andrea Lapi bought a house on this land from Bernardo Rossellino with the intention of turning it into a patrician manor. In 1630, the expansion was still unfinished.

Ornamental bust and vase on a balustrade in the 18th-century garden.

In 1718, the villa "in the place called La Gamberaia [the Crayfish Pond]" came into the possession of the Capponi family who further embellished it, giving the building its present-day aspect. The garden on the higher ground behind the villa, articulated with stairways and terraces and adorned with statues and rocaille motifs, also dates from the 17th and 18th centuries, as does the exedra with grotto and fountain situated at the end of the cypress-lined avenue leading up to the villa and the lemon-house.

The charming parterre with pools to one side of the villa, which terminates in an exedra formed of a massive, arcaded hedge,

Added to the villa's compact mass are flying arcades with walkways on top.

148

The front of the exedra in the north garden, decorated with bas-reliefs, rustic mosaics, and grotesques. was conceived by Princess Iohanna Ghyka and executed by gardeners Martino Porcinai and Luigi Messeri between 1905 and 1915.

Overleaf: The modern water parterre at Villa La Gamberaia, stretching towards an exedra of greenery and a lookout, with a view of Florence below.

The nymphaeum of the old garden behind Villa La Gamberaia, with its stone fountain and walls encrusted with "tartar," shells, and rough-hewn mosaics.

GARZONI
FAMILY

VILLA GARZONI
Collodi, Pistoia

Two extraordinary settings, each a contrast and complement to the other, combine to make this complex one of the most spectacular and magnificent sights offered by the repertory of Tuscan villas. On the one hand there is the "oversized" mass of the villa, which stands as a kind of a dike or dam restraining the vertiginous "cascade" of houses above it, perched on the slope of the old medieval village; on the other, there is the stately garden, which winds down in a series of terraces connected by stairways and ramps unfolding in a rhythmic sequence of diagonals.

In both cases it was the steep declivity of

Opposite: The palazzina d'estate, a summer pavilion designed by Juvarra that serves as a kind of link and transition in scale between the villa and the village behind it.

Right: The powerful mass of the villa seems to halt the cascade of houses in the old village of Collodi behind it.

Reception room at Villa Garzoni with grisaille or monochrome decorations and quadrature–illusionistic architectural views–on the ceiling by Angelo Michele Colonna, painted sometime before 1652.

the hillside that suggested the compositional arrangement of the various details and the whole splendid complex of Collodi. The villa and garden form a single unit of rare architectural efficacy harmonizing a series of vibrant spatial counterpoints; they are a convincing example of how artifice, if sufficiently bold in expressive intensity, can lend meaning to and enhance the natural surroundings.

An early image of what the Collodi complex would one day become is presented in a 1633 drawing executed for Romano Garzoni, who is generally given credit for building, and perhaps even designing, the first nucleus of the villa. This plan, in which there is no trace of the garden, shows a building realized through the enlargement of some existing structures but completed only up to the *piano nobile* and lacking, on the floor above, its central part.

From the descriptions given by Francesco Sbarra in *Le pompe di Collodi (The Splendors of Collodi)*, published in 1652, it appears that by this time some of the rooms had already been painted and that the great garden, which was "separate from the palace" and connected by a bridge spanning the torrent, had assumed some partially definitive shape.

In 1662, the villa's solid front was organically joined to the sloping terrain by the construction of a series of stepped access ramps that form a kind of bastion in front of it. Then in the late 18th century two bas-reliefs of trophies and banners were added to adorn the tops of the pilaster strips flanking the portal, which in those days also served as entrance to the village.

Around 1714 Filippo Juvarra presented his plans for the *palazzina d'estate*, or "summer house," to be built on a base of rusticated stone at the edge of the courtyard

behind the villa. This remarkable piece of architecture, conceived as a complex game of concave and convex surfaces, serves as a semicircular conclusion to the villa and a dramatic entry to the ancient village of Collodi.

The garden, on the other hand, was given its present shape in 1787 by the Luccan architect Ottaviano Diodati, "inventor and director of all the new works."

Diodati shaped his "water stairway or chain" according to the basic structure of the terraced hillside, crowning it at the top with the "proud terminus" of *Fame*, a statue attributed to Paladini of Lucca, and sealing it at the bottom of its sloping course with three straight walls in receding perspective, one above the other, with flights of stairs and balustraded landings.

Against the splendid backdrop of this formal triumph were arranged the bench-lined avenues, the hedgerows and thickets of cypress and bay laurel, the fountains, pools, maze, sculptures, the exedrae in mosaic, the ornamental waterworks, the rustic niches, the artificial rocks.

Antonio Cerati, member of the Accademia dell'Arcadia, was quite right when he wrote in 1783 that he considered Collodi "a metropolis among the Luccan villas, for the beauty, grandeur, and novelty it combines." And the aesthetic moments that make up this fabled "metropolis" can still be seen today, in the little theater of greenery, whose stage is adorned with statues of Thalia and Melpomenes; in the small pavilion intended "for ladies' and gentlemen's baths," situated at the top of the garden's incline; in the "paupers' lane" dotted with statues of beggars and commoners; in the "Avenue of the Four Seasons"; in the bridge between garden and villa, enclosed, like a tunnel, with high walls pierced by oval windows; in the grotto of the maze, adorned by the statue of a peasant emptying his barrel; and in the nymphaeum of Neptune, with its throng of agitated Tritons.

Other stone inhabitants of the garden include the flute-playing and cymbal-crashing *Fauns*, as well as *Flora, Diana, Bacchus, Apollo* and *Daphne,* and *Ceres,* which line the edge of the plaza of the "lower parterres"; and *Spring, Summer, Autumn,* and *Winter* housed in niches encrusted with sponge-like stone. Then

Opposite: Fame, a statue attributed to Paladini of Lucca, at the summit of the "water stairway" designed by Ottaviano Diodati for the garden at the Villa Garzoni.

Pescia Lucchese, an allegorical statue of the town of Pescia, at the bottom of the "water stairway."

Opposite: At Villa Garzoni, a perspective view of the three levels of stairs and terraced walls preceding the "water stairway." In the niche at the bottom is a terracotta statue, Peasant with a Barrel.

Statue of Apollo adorning the parterre at the entrance to the garden.

Detail of a balustrade and the mosaic decorations applied to a retaining wall on one of the garden terraces at Villa Garzoni.

there are the fountains entitled *Peasant with a Barrel and Peasant with a Turkey*; the twelve little terracotta monkeys in a variety of poses "expressing the game of *pallone*"; the many busts of Roman emperors; the satyrs leaning against the pilasters that border the third terrace at the foot of the "water stairway," and the winged dragons grazing at its base; the decorative spheres and vases crowning the various balustrades; Pomona with a lavish cornucopia; the matronly allegorical figures of the nearby town of Pescia, Pescia Toscana (with the Florentine lion) and Pescia Lucchese (with a dog); the solitary sculpture of a seated Turk, sole survivor of a *Caffehaus*; and the sculpture groups *Hercules* and the *Hydra* and *Samson Killing* the *Philistine*, which seem to compete in pride with the huge warriors and Amazons facing one another on the cornice topping off the villa's main façade.

The silent dialogues of this enchanted population scattered outside the palace are continued inside, on the vaults of the banquet halls and the walls of bedrooms and galleries, frescoed by the Bolognese Angelo Michele Colonna with quadrature (illusionistic architectural perspectives), views of ancient ruins, allegories, trophies, grisaille or monochrome busts of ancient Romans, and simulated statues of satyrs and putti. There are also bucolic scenes with figures of young peasants painted by other decorator-artists.

The illusionism of Colonna's frescoes, which broadens and transforms the static areas of the interior into a virtual space charged with Baroque energy, thus complements the spectacular aspects of the garden. This can be likened to a great piece of stage machinery, where mock wings, backdrops, and "mansions" come into view in real perspectives of height and depth that further transform themselves as the seasons change, and where the graceful build-up of architectural elements at different elevations effectively multiplies the spatial experience.

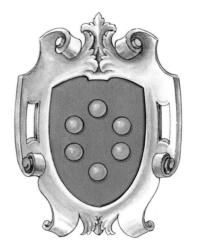

MANSI
FAMILY

COAT OF ARMS:
Azure six balls or in orle

VILLA MANSI
Segromigno, Lucca

An earlier building on this site, in the form of a horizontal parallelepiped, had belonged to the Benedetti family before being acquired by the Cenami in 1599. It was restructured in 1634-35 from plans by Muzio Oddi of Urbino, employed at the time by the Republic of Lucca as "Fortifications Engineer."

Commissioned by Countess Felice Cenami (who had the advice of her brother-in-law Paolo, in letters written from Paris), the rebuilding involved the addition to the south front of two projecting blocks joined by a portico not as deep as the new wings. The difference of depth allowed for the inclusion of the double staircase leading up to the portico. Above this a trabeated, three-bay loggia resting on coupled columns was erected, echoing the rhythms of the spatial division below.

Oddi's design clearly had two objectives in mind: to open the building to its surroundings with the airy, double loggias (which also command fine views); and to give volume to the façade through the hollow spaces enveloped by the same loggias.

Compared to these important architectural accomplishments, the building's stylistic and formal aspects fade into the background. They are hardly negligible, however, as we can see in the unusual repetition of the coupled-column motif (which would seem to give a sense of immateriality to the façade), or in the statues framed within each pair of columns and the masks and medallions placed between the extradoses of the arches. This assortment of motifs might have caused a compositional jumble, but the predominance of empty spaces over solid volumes succeeds in attenuating the apparent formal excess.

Such was the main façade of the villa

Overleaf: At Villa Mansi, a frontal view of the portico built in 1634-35 from plans by Muzio Oddi.

Side view of the main façade. The central upper section was added by the architect Giovan Francesco Giusti in 1742. There are 28 statues perched atop the upper balustrades around the villa, with another 8 adorning the portico and the old loggia above, not to mention numerous busts inserted in the window pediments on the piano nobile.

Central salone. On the wall is The Judgment of Midas *(1790) by Stefano Tofanelli. The grisaille painting on the ceiling and the illusionistic caryatids are also by Tofanelli.*

until 1742, when the Mansi, who had taken it over from the Cenami family in 1675, hired the architect Giovan Francesco Giusti to alter the upper story in front. Meanwhile, Filippo Juvarra of Messina had provided Ottavio Guido Mansi (in 1725) with plans

Bedroom at Villa Mansi with 18th-century canopy bed and walls painted with grottesche in the Pompeian style.

for the layout of the west garden, which was to supplement the east garden (dating from before 1684), and for the lovely Baroque

fish pond surrounded by a balustrade with statues.

As for the alteration of the south front, it must be said that Giusti, by enclosing the upper loggia, diminished the airy effect of the central part of the building. In compensation, however, he managed to lighten the appearance of the other wall masses by introducing supplementary elements, such as the balustrades inserted under some of the windows on all the façades, which gave them a finished quality, and to trim the crowning part of the old upper loggia. Moreover, the central gable he added (with pediment and an arch imitating the motif of the loggia below) gave a vertical thrust to the middle of the building and conferred a sense of greater solidity upon the whole.

Lessening the number of voids in the façade also strengthened and enhanced the spatial role of the lower loggia and highlighted the function of the statues, which were intended to animate the wall surfaces. As a further instance of this sculptural motif, Giusti, in redesigning the frames of the windows on the main floor, placed male and female busts in the pediments.

Inside the villa, the salone, which runs from the front to the back of the building and represents the center of domestic life, was decorated in the late 18th century by the Lucchese painter Stefano Tofanelli with scenes from the life of Apollo in a setting of illusionistic architecture, all fresco-painted.

In the 19th century, the central part of the rear façade was raised one story. Around the same time, Juvarra's garden was almost entirely destroyed in order to create something more "natural."

A unicorn, an elephant, a crocodile, two sphinxes, and some parrots are among the exotic elements in this grotesque adorning a wall in the Villa Mansi dining room.

*The great lawn in front of
the Villa Mansi, seen from
inside the portico.*

175

CORSI
FAMILY

COAT OF ARMS:
Party per bend gules and vert a bend argent, a lion rampant vert on gules and gules on vert

VILLA CORSI
Sesto Fiorentino, Florence

Right: Façade looking onto the garden.

Below: A corner of the garden with two marble statues.

In 1502, Simone di Jacopo Corsi bought "an estate . . . with a manor house and service quarters" in the "parish of San Martino at Sesto" from Luca di Andrea Carnesecchi. He probably renovated this "manor house" to look like a small country palace, an aspect further emphasized by the work done on it by his son Giovanni in 1567 and 1569.

The results of these alterations are presumably visible in the two illustrations of the house (commissioned by Giovanni himself) to be found among the grottesche adorning one of the rooms. Attributed to

Alessandro del Barbiere, these paintings show the main façade (with the stone bench along the base of the building, statues of dogs lodged in niches and guarding the entranceway, trabeated windows, covered roof-terrace, and dovecote), and a view of the inner courtyard with a fountain and an arcade opening onto an unspecified landscape.

A second phase of renovation took place roughly between 1593 and 1603, at the instigation of Giovanni's heirs. However, the major transformation of the country palazzetto into a villa proper took place from 1632 to 1641 and involved an enlargement of the building and the construction of a garden.

The villa's principal design, dominated by four crenelated towers at the corners, presumably dates from this period as does the layout of the garden, which is divided into geometric segments and features a round pool at its center, flower beds bordered by wild box, a fish pond, kitchen garden, and citrus greenhouse.

All this was restructured yet again, and in a coherent fashion, by Antonio Corsi in 1738. On that occasion the façades were entirely redefined, their surfaces divided by pilaster strips running the full height of the building. This left, on the rear façade overlooking the garden, two higher stories (corresponding to the 17th-century towers), which were adorned with elegant Serlianas (triple openings, the central one arched and wider than the other two) and balustrades. The two towers facing the road were destroyed, while at the center of the façade a high gable with scrolls, trimmed with obelisk-shaped pinnacles, was added. Lastly, all the façades were crowned with continuous balustrades, and a number of decorative statues were placed at the top of the garden front.

The villa's new face found a perfect counterpart in the contemporary adjustments made to the garden. The aviaries were decorated and joined together by a wall with a central opening surmounted by a pediment; the long

178

179

Wall fresco of landscape viewed through an Egyptian revival colonnade.

rectangular pool was rebuilt and appropriately adorned with balusters and effigies of the Four Seasons; the boundary wall was redesigned with pilasters, scroll profiles, ornamental vases, and statues of rustic subjects; and the canal with cascades along the avenue of the grove was constructed.

The relationship of villa to garden was likewise enhanced by the external projections (loggias and balconies), which still look out today onto the greenery below,

181

Terracotta Cerberus atop the garden wall at Villa Corsi.

and by the formal harmony between the marble and terracotta sculptures adorning the building and those on the ground that mark off the segments of the parterre. The consistent ratio, numerically and formally, between the statues arranged on the vertical surfaces and those spread out over the horizontal plane constitutes one of the most outstanding features of this villa in its 18th-century aspect, a characteristic also brought out in Giuseppe Zocchi's famous engraving of it. Inside the villa, in addition to the little room with a frescoed vault of grottesche around the two images of the Cinquecento palazzetto and the Cupid and Psyche in the central panel, there are numerous other rooms with wall paintings. Their subjects range from 19th-century allegories of the Four Elements to an illusionistic Egyptian-revival colonnade.

VILLA L'UGOLINO
Florence

UGOLINI
FAMILY

COAT OF ARMS:
Party per bend, or and azure, a
leopard azure with bezants or
in chief, a leopard or with
roundels azure in base

Originally a modest manor house belonging to Piero di Cristofano di Domenico da Montevarchi, this structure was acquired by the Lotti family in 1427 and then sold to Giorgio di Niccolò Ugolini in 1444. It was the Ugolini who saw to the transformation of the old casa da signore into a villa.

Around the year 1645, Giovanni Sini, biographer of the architect and sculptor Gherardo Silvani, wrote that near Strada, on the Via Chiantigiana, Silvani had completed for Bartolomeo Ugolini a palazzo "of great magnificence . . . begun by his teacher Giovanni Caccini."

While the features of the structure built by Caccini are no longer visible, the modest results of Silvani's intervention can be assessed, especially on the villa's rear façade. In general, they amount to an outdated typological repertory of Mannerist forms (such as the rusticated portal and the windows with gratings curving outward at the bottom).

Much livelier and more energetic in its forms and articulations of space is the caisson-patterned façade giving onto the Via Chiantigiana; its deep triple-arched portico with a central flight of steps is an addition dating from 1714. Unfortunately, the original appearance of this façade has been ruined by the walling up of nearly all the windows.

In 1744, Giorgio Ugolini had the entire building restored. It was probably on that occasion that the chapel of Saints Francis and Francesca Romana was built inside the villa.

The residential rooms are positioned around the two-story central salone on the ground floor. In 1691, the walls and ceiling of this great hall were decorated with allegorical and pastoral scenes by Atanasio Bimbacci.

The Rape of Persephone, frescoed on the vault of the central salone at Villa L'Ugolino by the Florentine artist Atanasio Bimbacci in 1691. To the right is the Ugolini coat of arms, though here it is "party azure and or" rather than "party or and azure."

VILLA BURLAMACCHI
Gattaiola, Lucca

BURLAMACCHI
FAMILY

COAT OF ARMS:
Or a cross azure

Opposite: An oblique view of the villa gives a clear sense of its cubical shape.

Below: The loggia at the rear of the house, with vaults and walls decorated by the Lucchese painter Francesco Antonio Cecchi.

Begun by Francesco Burlamacchi (from plans most likely drafted by the school of Nicolao Civitali), this building had been completed as far as the vaults of the second story in 1556. The villa's austere typology, an undistinguished cubical form embellished only by a seven-bay loggia on the ground floor of the rear façade, gives little indication of the imaginative and lavish frescoes inside. These decorations were initiated in the 17th century by the Santini family, who replaced the Burlamacchi, and continued in the 18th century under the Montecatini, who replaced the Santini in their turn.

The *quadrature* or trompe-l'oeil architectural perspectives painted on the walls and ceilings–which create an illusory expansion of space–transformed the appearance of the traditionally shaped rooms. The most effective of these eye-fooling frescoes are those by Bartolomeo di Santi of Lucca, who created faux pilasters framing niches, statues, arches, and balconies. He also endowed the vault of one room with the image of a great portico opening onto a sky crossed by the Chariot of the Sun, the Hours, Dawn, Time, and Spring. In an adjoining room, the perspective created by a continuous balustrade bulging outward at the corners bursts right through the curvatures of the ceiling.

Illusionistic niches with monochrome busts of allegories painted by Francesco Antonio Cecchi adorn the rear loggia, which in 1719 was given a double staircase. And imaginary landscapes, serving as backgrounds to episodes of Tasso's *Jerusalem Delivered* and bucolic scenes, enrich the walls of still other rooms.

What is remarkable about this villa is not, therefore, its architecture, but rather its great store of decorative painting. It is hardly a surprise that one of its 19th-century owners should have been Count Alfred Emilien Nieuwerkerke, "*l'homme le plus décoré, plus décorateur, plus décoratif*" ("the most decorated, decorating, and decorative of men"), who is suspected of having destroyed the garden and circular hedge-maze of Gattaiola (to replace it with an English-style garden) but is also remembered as a sculptor, director-general of French museums, organizer of the famous *vendredis du Louvre*, and later Superintendent of Fine Arts under Napoleon III.

Right: Ceiling of the
ballroom of Villa
Burlamacchi, with
illusionistic architecture
and The Chariot of the Sun
painted by Bartolomeo di
Santi.

Painting of a statue, a
detail of the wall
decorations commissioned
by the Santini family for the
ballroom.

Opposite: Detail of the wall paintings executed by Bartolomeo di Santi in the ballroom at Villa Burlamacchi.

Small room adjoining the ballroom. On the walls are panels with views of architectural structures and ancient ruins.

VILLA DI CELLE
Pistoia

FABRONI
FAMILY

COAT OF ARMS:
Azure a bend or charged with
three hammers sable, with ball
argent a cross gules in sinister
chief

*The majestic façade of the
villa, seen from the plaza in
front.*

Situated on the "Montale Hill," this
magnificent residence was built by the
Fabroni family during the 17th century and
incorporates some earlier fortified
structures.

Rising four stories above the ground, the
villa is connected inside from floor to floor
by two curvilinear staircases leading down

194

Opposite: In this room at the Villa di Celle the vaults painted in grottesche serve as a pleasantly contrasting context for a bronze statue by Marino Marini, a sculpture by Henry Moore, a painting by Roy Lichtenstein, and other contemporary works of art.

Below: Grisaille wall paintings from the Neoclassical period give this room its particular flavor and set off Manzù's Little Cardinal and a painting by Léger.

to the front plaza. This great forecourt centers around the fountain at the middle of a circular pool guarded by pairs of sculpted dolphins. A double stairway outside connects the plaza to the building's imposing façade, which is distinguished by four rusticated pilaster strips and by molded panels, and culminates in an undulant gable end.

The front plaza also serves as a vast, open atrium to the park created in 1844-45 by the Caselli Counts, who replaced the Fabroni. Especially Romantic, and in marked contrast to the solemn exterior of the villa, is the section of the park designed by Giovanni Gambini of Pistoia, who, "once he had finished the island and the surroundings of the lake, conceived, directed, and realized [this area] in natural forms, without the contrivances of art." Also by Gambini are the grotto, the waterfall and artificial cliff, the "Egyptian" monument, the rustic cottage, the pavilion and other elements nearby that were intended to supplement the octagonal, pagoda-shaped aviary designed by Bartolomeo Sestini in 1812. The Gothic-revival *palazzina*, was built by Ferdinando Marini.

These Romantic park ornaments complemented the earlier terracotta lions crouching at the tops of the pilasters of the garden gate, as well as the statue of the goddess Pomona and the bas-relief of the Battle of the Tritons on the wall of the wall of the orchard pool.

Today all these creations live side by side with the modern attractions added by the current owner of the property, Giuliano Gori: the labyrinth by Morris, the astrolabes of Oppenheim, was well as works by Nagasawa, Kosuth, Aycock, Serra, Burri, Poirier, and others. With them the Celle park has become a kind of a museum of avant-garde art.

VILLA LA PIETRA
Florence

A manor house on this site, belonging to the Macinghi family, was sold to the Sassetti family in 1460 and then acquired by the Capponi in 1546. In the first half of the 1600s, Cardinal Luigi Capponi, had this house converted into a villa.

The renovation ordered by the Cardinal also included changing the original courtyard into a round, two-story *salone* encircled on the inside by a curving staircase. Further alterations were made on the building after 1697, by Senator Alessandro Capponi, who for this task probably employed the Roman architect Carlo Fontana and the Florentine engineer Alessandro Cecchini, the same men who erected a *palazzo* for Capponi in Florence between 1702 and 1710.

It is nevertheless difficult to find much similarity between the architectural elements, internal and external, of the palace and Villa La Pietra, except perhaps in the general use of a fluent formal language and in the solidity of mass. In this, however,

Right: Rear façade, seen from the Italian-style garden.

Opposite: Detail of the balustraded staircase and terrace at the base of the south front.

Opposite: The "rotunda" at Villa La Pietra (created from the original courtyard), distinguished by its airy staircase and Mannerist fountain with the figure of a satyr.

Left: The furnishings of this room, with Cinquecento tapestries, Oriental vases and screen, and 18th-century chairs, successfully combine eclectic antiquarian tastes.

203

the villa resembles an urban *palazzo* of that period, the most distinguishing feature of which was the great number of windows looking onto the public street.

The villa-like aspect of this building derives above all from its secluded location in the hills of Florence, and from the layout of its garden, realized after 1904 by its proprietor at the time. This was Arthur Acton, an English art dealer who planted rows of cypresses and created a terraced green space in the manner of an "Italian garden," basing it on traditional models and adorning it with 17th- and 18th-

century statues from the Veneto (by the sculptors Orazio Marinali and Francesco Bonazza).

The building's interior–as is often true–shows more characteristics in keeping with the villa prototype. A case in point would be the antechamber with frescoed landscapes featuring ruins and skies dotted with birds and Cupids, or the upper section of the central *salone* with frescoes of figures in 18th-century dress and illusionistic sculptural groups against porticoed backgrounds.

Another charming corner of the garden at Villa La Pietra, with balustrades, statues, and an archway at the end acting as backdrop to a stage of greenery.

VILLA CHIGI
Cetinale, Siena

CHIGI
DELLA ROVERE
FAMILY

COAT OF ARMS:
Quartered, 1st and 4th azure
with uprooted oak of four
branches or in two decussate
crosses (Della Rovere), 2nd
and 3rd gules a mountain of
six peaks or, surmounted by an
eight-pointed star or (Chigi)

Cardinal Flavio Chigi, nephew of Pope Alexander VII, engaged the Roman architect Carlo Fontana to design this villa, on which construction began in 1680.

The external elegance of the building's

*Page 208: The main façade
of Villa Chigi as seen
at the end of the avenue
of cypresses.
In the foreground are the
two architectural features
marking the entrance.*

*Pages 208-209: The south
façade of Villa Chigi, with
its double loggia and
projecting wings, is in type
somewhat reminiscent of
Baldassarre Peruzzi's Villa
Le Volte.*

compact volume derives from the contrast between the brickwork framing its arches and windows and the vertical stone quoins that mark its corners. Roman influences can be seen in the majestic arrangement of the double stairway on the main façade and in the two small, faceted walls, adorned with obelisks and statues carved by Bartolomeo Mazzuoli, that mark the entrance to the avenue of cypresses leading up to the villa.

A bas-relief inside the villa, representing Cardinal Flavio Chigi receiving Cosimo III de' Medici at Cetinale in 1691, is also by Mazzuoli.

Opposite the avenue of cypress, a steeply inclined rectilinear stairway leads up to a secluded hermitage, the central niche of which is occupied by a great patriarchal cross (with two crossbeams) with busts of saints at its extremities. Perched atop a hill, this retreat symbolizes—both topographically and in terms of anchoritic expiation—the highest point and the farthest limit of the Park of the Hermitage below.

Writing of the motives that led Cardinal Chigi to create this park, Joseph Forsyth observed in 1816 that "Cetinale . . . owes its fame to the remorse of a libertine Cardinal who, to placate the ghost of a murdered rival, transformed a gloomy cypress plantation into a penitential retreat, where he subjected himself to all the harsh discipline of an Egyptian hermit."

Regardless of the veracity of this information, it is easy to appreciate the exceptional quality of the park, which is dotted with small chapels, crisscrossed by paths, and inhabited with statues of monsters and animals (sculpted by Mazzuoli).

Popular tradition has identified these as representing the insignias of the various *contrade* of Siena participating in the famous Palio horse race in that city.

The gallery with walls and vaults painted with landscape motifs and illusionistic arbors.

211

VILLA CORSINI
Castello, Florence

In 1618, Cosimo II de' Medici acquired a *palazzetto* that in the 15th century had belonged to the Strozzi family before being sold in 1460 to Bernardo di Stoldo Rinieri. In 1650, the Office of Royal Possessions transferred it to Piero di Bernardo Cervini. Finally, after several other changes of ownership, it was bought by Lucrezia Rinuccini, wife of Marquess Filippo Corsini, in 1697.

From the contract drawn up between the Strozzi and the Rinieri we know that the object of sale was an "estate with a manor house and service quarters." In all likelihood, the transformation of this multifunctional structure into a villa was carried out by the Rinieri in the mid-1500s. Probably datable to this period are the inner courtyard with arcades on three sides (with Ionic columns) and the garden ornaments, which include "a life-size river god in gray stone spouting water into a great basin of the same stone," sculpted by Tribolo and positioned in a niche "atop a grove" (as recalled by Vasari), and a marble boy spouting water from his "virile member," carved by Pierino da Vinci and situated above a "stone basin." (Both sculptors were also working at the time on the "fountains of the Duke" at the nearby Medici villa of Castello.)

It was the Corsini who commissioned the later renovations, executed between 1690 and 1700, which gave the villa its present form. The plans for these alterations have been attributed by some to the architect Antonio Ferri, who from 1695 to 1697 was working on a *palazzo* in Florence for the same family. There is not enough documentation to support this attribution, however, and in fact it seems more likely, on the evidence of a drawing by Giovan Battista Foggini of one view of the inner courtyard, that it was Foggini (also active in the works at Palazzo Corsini) who transformed the villa's inner and outer appearance by means of a number of superficial Baroque features. The ornamentation of the main façade (i.e., the lively volutes of the window pediments) and the stuccowork in the reception hall seem particularly reminiscent of decorative motifs present in some of Foggini's other Florentine projects (such as the *salone* of Palazzo Viviani and the interiors of the churches of San Giorgio and Santo Spirito alla Costa). In any case, the long, asymmetrical front of the Corsini country palace (looking onto the Via della Petraia), with its rhythm of pilaster strips dividing the façade and the majestic gable that vertically extends the central segment, undoubtedly constitutes one of the richest and most stylistically unified architectural expressions to be found among the villas of Tuscany.

The reception hall, two stories high, is graced by elevated openings (windows with balconies and a small gallery) and by lavish fresco decorations. Its vaulted ceiling displays a triumph of angels upholding the Corsini-Rinuccini coat of arms.

The French-style garden to the side of the villa is noteworthy for its spectacular arrangement of stairways and balustrades that fan out from the so-called "Horse Fountain" springing from a great scroll of stone.

The garden "of the four seasons," extending in a semicircle in front of the villa's secondary façade, is punctuated by rocaille pedestals supporting statues and ornamental vases.

Opposite: Detail of the central segment of the main façade.

The 18th-century Horse Fountain in the French garden.

215

VILLA DI LAPPEGGI
Grassina, Florence

MEDICI
FAMILY

COAT OF ARMS
(after 1469,
with grand-ducal crown):
Or a six balls in orle, five gules
and one azure in chief, charged
with three fleurs-de-lis

*Opposite: Room with
quadratura wall paintings
and lunettes frescoed with
portraits of Medici princes.*

*Below: Giusto Utens, View
of Villa di Lappeggi, late
16th century, Museo di
Firenze com'era, Florence.
In 1814, the precarious
state of the building led to
the demolition of the two
top floors.*

In 1513, the Gualtierotti family bought a turreted house from the Bardi in a place called "Appeggi" or "Lappeggi." In 1551, they sold it to the Bartolini Salimbeni, who transferred it in turn to the Ricasoli family in 1560.

Attracted by the advantages of the site, Prince Ferdinando de' Medici bought the building from the Ricasoli in 1569 and upon becoming Grand Duke had it transformed into a villa, confiding the task (which was completed in 1585) to Bernardo Buontalenti. The depiction of the villa in the lunette painted by Giusto Utens between 1559 and 1602 shows a building modeled on the Peruzzian prototype of Le Volte in Siena, taken up again by the Florentine Villa I Collazzi: a U-shaped design with the central façade characterized by two loggias, one above the other.

The significance of this typology–open to the surrounding landscape, which is

LA PEGGIO

219

Page 218: Alessandro Gherardini's Allegory of Time (1703) at Villa di Lappeggi.

Page 219: Wall headboard in the so-called "Cardinal's Room" on the ground floor. The gilded stucco putti and drapery were executed by Giovan Battista Ciceri in 1702. The Annunciation (1703) is attributed to Alessandro Gherardini.

Opposite: Ground-floor banquet hall at Villa di Lappeggi. On the ceiling is a fresco of 1703 by Pier Dandini. The quadrature on the walls are by Rinaldo Botti.

embraced by the projecting wings–was, however, partially negated by the presence of a high, crenelated wall hemming in the space in front of the closed courtyard. Peruzzi's concept, not fully grasped by Buontalenti, was later recovered and even enhanced by Antonio Ferri who, beginning in 1698, opened the courtyard up to the garden by creating a semicircular front terrace from which two elegant curvilinear stairways descended.

This project, as well as the renovation of the building's interior, was commissioned by Cardinal Francesco Maria de' Medici, to whom the villa had been transferred in 1667 by his brother Cosimo III. Earlier, it had been given in usufruct to the Orsini, reacquired by the Grand Dukes of Tuscany, bequeathed to Prince Don Mattias de' Medici, and inherited by Cosimo III. An 18th-century drawing by Giuseppe Zocchi makes it possible to evaluate the results of Ferri's efforts, which included a reorganization of the garden. Outer avenues bordering the parterres were created; flower beds were laid out in symmetrical patterns; fountains and small nymphaea were built; and allegorical statues of rivers were placed on either side of the grotto at the base of the double stairway leading up to the villa.

The villa's interior, some of which had been decorated at the time of Don Mattias, was further embellished in 1702-03 by the frescoes of Pier Dandini and Alessandro Gherardini, the *quadratura* perspectives of Rinaldo Botti and Giuseppe Tonelli, and the stuccowork of Giovan Battista Ciceri.

By 1708, once the decorations–which had brought together the finest Florentine craftsmen of the period–were complete, the villa could be seen as an "18th-century Pratolino," with a theater, *Caffehaus*, and a place set aside for the game of *pallacorda* (the early Italian version of tennis). As such

Ground-floor banquet hall at Villa di Lappeggi, with a detail of Rinaldo Botti's quadrature of 1703. The simulated atlantes were probably painted by Pier Dandini.

it was the perfect setting for receiving the court of "eccentric spirits" led by the poet Giovan Battista Fagioli, and for meeting the needs of the pleasure-loving Medici Cardinal, who has been called a "bon viveur par excellence" and "corrupt by nature."

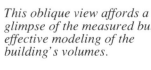

VILLA DI POGGIO TORSELLI
San Casciano Val di Pesa, Florence

ORLANDINI
FAMILY

COAT OF ARMS:
Azure three rams argent
rampant, contrarampant in
chief, with triple-dovetailed
label gules in chief

In his *Life* of the Florentine sculptor and architect Lorenzo Merlini, Francesco Saverio Baldinucci writes: "Upon his return to Florence in 1702, [Merlini] built from the foundations a villa palace at Poggio Torselli for signor Gio-Battista Orlandini, which remained unfinished owing to that gentleman's death."

A patron of the arts and member of the Accademia del Disegno, Giovan Battista di Girolamo Corsini, who acquired the new surname Orlandini in 1644, was apparently pleased with the architect's work, since shortly thereafter he hired him to sculpt two allegorical statues for the family chapel in the Florentine church of Santa Maria Maggiore. Merlini's work had also won the confidence and appreciation of the Florentine nobility in general, as witnessed by the commissions he was granted to "expand and restore" the palazzo of Senator Carlo Ginori, the villas of Marquess Pier Antonio Gerini at Le Maschere and of Marquess Acciaioli at Montegufoni, and the Palazzi Dati and Bagnano.

The villa at Poggio Torselli is further proof that the confidence shown in Merlini was clearly deserved. The architect in fact managed to impart a stately energy to the exterior by grafting two unobtrusive wings onto each side, and by complementing the main façade with the slightly projecting middle segment (crowned by statues), which is joined to the lateral walls by broad, concave pilaster strips running the entire height of the building. These create an unusually soft, "shell-like" juncture reminiscent of Pietro da Cortona. The villa's interior has its own share of surprises. Foremost among these are the noteworthy formal effect of the staircase, and the exquisite fresco decorations by Matteo Bonechi and his pupils.

This oblique view affords a glimpse of the measured but effective modeling of the building's volumes.

Opposite: Allegorical figures on a bedroom ceiling in Villa di Poggio Torselli, painted by Matteo Bonechi.

The liveliest spatial experience inside the villa is offered by the great staircase, with its fluid succession of flights, landings, and vaults.

VILLA SANTINI
Camigliano, Lucca

SANTINI
FAMILY

COAT OF ARMS:
Azure two lozenges argent, a
rose gules in chief

An earlier building on this site, dating from the second half of the 16th century, was purchased in 1651 by Nicolao Santini. Some time before 1710, he had the front part enlarged and renovated by adding a substantial new façade, which, for the entire height of the first story, is linked up to the rest of the house on either side by masonry

With its dramatic rise toward a majestic crescendo–underscored by the gradual diminution of the width, the sequential receding of the three stories, and the final thrust of the domed turret–this façade radically redefines the earlier structure by situating it in a pulsating, polychrome frame. This effect is cadenced by the

Above: The Garden of Flora with the protruding dome of the grotto, crowned by scrolls and grotesque masks and culminating in the statue of Flora.

Right: Detail of the fish-pond balustrade. The Mermaid beyond is a stone sculpture by Matraia.

of alternating smooth and rusticated courses and voussoirs. The man who designed this addition, which effectively defines the villa's appearance, was the Bolognese Alfonso Torregiani. In fact, in compositional and formal terms, his façade stands as one of the most articulate and important achievements among all the villas of Tuscany, comparable only to the main front of Villa Mansi at Segromigno.

Page 229: At Villa Santini,
a raking view of the main
façade highlights the play
of projections and recesses.

A statue of Hercules and
Cerberus in a niche at the
entrance to the octagonal
grotto in the Garden of
Flora.

accumulation of arches and balustrades, the
array of marble statues, the alternating rows
of rough yellow tufa and gray ashlar, the
cavities of the niches and ovals, the deep
empty spaces behind the Serlian-motif
openings at the center, and the multiplicity
of flat and projecting surfaces. To speak of a
façade in this instance is almost

inappropriate, inasmuch as the space
enveloping and traversing the building's
entire front tends to collect in the openings,
thicken in the hollows, condense around the
statues, and find its shape according to the
differences of level.

This external exuberance is echoed
inside the villa as well, in the forms

Overleaf: The colorful
main façade displays an
elaborate articulation of
forms and a lavish array of
more than forty statues.

enveloping the two elliptical staircases, and
(in a manner more simulated than real) in
the Aureliano room with its stuccowork, its
trompe-l'oeil architectural perspectives by
the Lucchese *quadraturista* Pietro Scorzini,
and its ceiling fresco of an aerial
Apotheosis painted by the Florentine
Vincenzo Dandini.

At the same time the villa was being
renovated, the Garden of Flora was being
put together. This included an elegant
four-flight stairway (leading up to the level
of the fish pond) and a nymphaeum with a
domed grotto, crowned by scrolls
supporting the canephore, a statue of Flora
with a basket on her head.

Serving as backdrop to the
Garden of Flora at Villa
Santini, this elegant
stairway leads to a higher
level of the park laid out
around a rectangular fish
pond.

MALASPINA
FAMILY

COAT OF ARMS:
Party per fess gules and or, a
briar plant proper uprooted,
with five flowers argent

VILLA MALASPINA
Caniparola di Fosdinovo,
Massa Carrara

Around 1720, Carlo Agostino Malaspina, Marquess of Fosdinovo, and his son Gabriello built this elegant villa on a spot where–according to Emanuele Repetti–there once stood an ancient tower.

On the outside, the building displays rather unusual architectural characteristics. Careful examination of the main façade enables the viewer to note and appreciate the way in which the two parallel rows of openings are separated by means of a broad band of solid wall. The diminishing height of the façade's three sections (two of which are pierced) as they rise from the paneled base creates a dynamic sequence that enlivens the horizontal structure of the whole. Indeed, the final, narrow band of the attic, with its central gable resting on long volutes, only accentuates the horizontality of the villa's front.

Still other details add to one's appreciation of the compositional brilliance of this façade. For example, the greater width of the loggia's central arch is echoed twice: below by the splaying of the steps past the first landing, and above by the broader, arched opening that breaks up the formal rhythm of the square windows. Since these rest on a continuous sill line, the little balcony of the central window is dropped to a slightly lower level.

To the features just cited, which have thus far involved two-dimensional space, must be added the depth of the loggia and the recessed window casings. Such differences of depth lend substance and spatial density to the entire façade.

Aside from these strictly architectonic qualities, the villa's exterior also displays lively coloring, a testimony to the Ligurian influences that, not surprisingly in a border region such as this, have here successfully combined with Tuscan formal traditions.

Right: The main façade, seen from the garden in bloom.

Pages 236-237: The two-story ballroom frescoed with quadrature in 1728 by Giovan Battista Natali, known as Il Piacentino. To the right, the trompe-l'oeil doorway offers the receding perspective of a majestic staircase.

*Opposite: Dining room in
Villa Malaspina with an
18th-century fireplace in
white Carrara marble. On
the walls are illusionistic
architectural motifs and
trompe-l' oeil backgrounds.*

*Bedroom on the piano
nobile, with canopy bed and
period tapestries and
furniture.*

VILLA LA TANA
Candeli, Florence

RICASOLI FIRIDOLFI
FAMILY

COAT OF ARMS:
Quartered, 1st barry or and
gules, a lion rampant azure
(Ricasoli); 2nd or a castle
proper (Baron Ricasoli); 3rd
argent a bend gules charged of
a mullet or in chief (Firidolfi);
4th paly gules and or debruised
of three bars azure

*Right: Entrance stairway
and façade, seen from
below, a view that
heightens the spectacular
effect of the whole.*

*Below: The terrace in front
of the villa, with the
Florentine plain below.*

In 1631, Baron Giulio Ricasoli
purchased a *casa da signore* in the district
of Candeli from the Hospital of Santa Maria
Nuova in Florence. The house had
previously belonged to the "most excellent
lady Bianca Cappello, a Venetian
aristocrat."

Signora Cappello, mistress of Grand
Duke Francesco I de' Medici, had come
into full possession of the property after the
death of her husband, Piero Zanobi
Bonaventuri, in 1574. Bonaventuri had
bought it in 1570 from the Landi family,
who had acquired it from the Bucelli in
1548.

It was the Ricasoli, however, who, with
timely enlargements and embellishments,
made a villa of the existing manor house,
called *La Tana* ("The Hideaway"), because
it was originally "almost hidden in the wood
that covered the entire side of the hill of the
Incontro."

According to Francesco Saverio

At Villa La Tana, a detail of one of the curved flights of the entrance stairway, on which the terracotta statues confer a certain solemnity.

Opposite: At Villa La Tana, a detail of the grotto of Poseidon built into the front of the entrance stairway. Encrustations of sponge-like stone, shells, and rough-hewn mosaics make up the décor.

Below: The hills around Poggio delle Tortore, seen through the loggia that connects the villa to the east garden.

Right: Aerial view of Villa La Tana and its outbuildings. At the top is a stretch of the Arno, near the weir of Le Viacce.

Baldinucci, the renovations commissioned in 1740 by Leon Francesco Pasquale Ricasoli were designed by the architect Giulio Foggini, brother of the more famous Giovan Battista Foggini. Foggini's work yielded an edifice that, thanks in part to its situation on a hillside, is one of the most spectacular of its kind in Tuscany.

Indeed, the villa's front, with its two lower side wings and an attic that assumes the prominence of a gable, rises majestically above an imposing sequence of stairs that begins with the broad, semicircular flight of steps at the bottom. The two curvilinear, pincer-like arms of the main stairway frame a grotto at the center of the wall retaining the convergent, rectilinear extensions of the stairs.

The parallel sequence of statues erected in later years on the bannisters confer a sense of solemnity on this ascending path to the terrace-lookout in front of the villa, which affords a view of Florence.

A comparison of the villa's current aspect with Giuseppe Zocchi's 18th-century *veduta* ("view") shows that the main façade underwent changes in the 19th century that altered the composition of pilaster strips and windows and eliminated the charming mixtilinear panel decorations.

The interior revolves compositionally around the two-story *salone*, which is surrounded by elevated galleries and was decorated in 1722 with paintings of seascapes by Antonio Cioci.

The present garden, on the other hand, with its geometric parterres, walls, and exedrae of greenery, is the result of recent landscaping inspired by 18th-century models.

BIANCHI BANDINELLI PAPARONI
FAMILY

COAT OF ARMS:
Party per pale; 1st arabesqued or a roundel azure in sinister canton of chief, charged of an armed knight argent on a horse courant of same (Bandinelli Paparoni); 2nd azure a sword upright argent surmounted of three stars or, one in chief and one each to the side

One of the six monumental gates that serve as entrances to the garden.

VILLA BIANCHI BANDINELLI
Geggiano, Siena

In describing this building, which originally was probably a farmhouse with masters' quarters, the well-known scholar Ranuccio Bianchi Bandinelli (who died in 1975) tells how it came into his family's possession "as part of the dowry of Girolama Santi, the first wife of Ranuccio Bandinelli Paparoni." He adds that "in 1729, the various parts of the old structure were joined together, one room was added to each floor on the left side, and a loggia, now closed, was added to either side. This gave the villa the structure it still has today."

Yet its present-day appearance, as Bianchi Bandinelli points out, "derives essentially from the renovations made between 1768 and 1779, which have remained for the most part unaltered."

This appearance features a façade with a vertical sequence of pilaster strips crossed at the level of the *piano nobile* by a horizontal fascia comprising the parallel lines of the stringcourse and the window sills.

In the 19th century, as is evidenced in a drawing by Ettore Romagnoli, a large, decorated, round-headed gable (as wide as the central section of the façade) covered the front of the attic.

The modest forms of the exterior give little indication of the sumptuous interior, redecorated "in the 18th-century style" between 1780 and 1790 and graced with furniture expressly designed by the Sienese architect Agostino Fantastici–the canopy bed, for example, and tables with caryatids. Illusionistic paintings of tapestries on the walls of the Green Room depict farm work corresponding to the seasons. The allegories of the months of the year, painted in fresco in the long entrance gallery, are by the Tyrolean artist Ignatius Moder, who was active in Siena at the time.

The Italian garden that begins at the edge of the forecourt features an 18th-century open-air theater with masonry proscenium and semicircular wings of greenery. The two parts of the proscenium consist of arches surmounted by triumphal pediments, bearing the coats of arms of the Bianchi Bandinelli and Chigi Zondadari families, and diagonal walls with niches holding statues of Comedy and Tragedy, carved by the Maltese sculptor Bosio. The garden is surrounded by a wall with six different gates, each flanked by monumental pillars with finely stepped moldings at the top, crowned by ornamental vases and terracotta monkeys.

The Green Room in Villa Bianchi Bandinelli. The walls are painted with faux tapestries representing the Seasons. The ceiling frescoes contain amusing scenes entitled "Wife-Hunting" and "Husband-Fishing."

*Two details of the wall
paintings in the entrance
gallery at Villa Bianchi
Bandinelli, executed by
Ignatius Moder in 1799.
The small horse on wheels
to the far right is an old toy.*

MEDICI
FAMILY

COAT OF ARMS
(after 1469, with grand-ducal crown):
Or six balls in orle, five gules and one azure in chief, charged with three fleurs-de-lis

LORRAINE
FAMILY

COAT OF ARMS:
Tierced in pale; 1st or a bend gules charged of three alerions argent (Lorraine); 2nd gules a fess argent (Austria); 3rd or six balls in orle, five gules and one azure in chief, charged of three fleurs-de-lis

Far right: Central section of the main façade. Below is Pasquale Poccianti's rusticated portico; above, the loggia added by Giuseppe Cacialli.

Right: Statue of Hercules bearing the heavens, by Vincenzo de' Rossi.

VILLA DEL POGGIO IMPERIALE
Florence

In 1487, a manor house on the Arcetri hill belonging to the Baroncelli family was transferred to the Pandolfini, who in 1548 sold it to Piero Salviati.

Confiscated in 1565 by Grand Duke Cosimo I de' Medici and given as a gift to his daughter Isabella (as part of the dowry she brought to Paolo Orsini), the house eventually came into the possession of the Odescalchi family, who in 1622 sold it to Grand Duchess Maria Maddalena of Austria, wife of Cosimo II.

For the "restoration, enlargement, and embellishment" of the existing building, the

Page 260: One wall of the peristyle designed by Cacialli for the piano nobile at Villa del Poggio Imperiale. The stucco decorations are by Spedulo and Marinelli.

Page 261: View of the peristyle built at the time of Elisa Baciocchi. The landscapes depicting the Four Seasons are by Giuseppe Gherardi.

Left: Central courtyard redesigned by Giovan Battista Foggini around 1690 for Grand Duchess Vittoria Della Rovere.

Grand Duchess sponsored a competition that involved the architects Gherardo Silvani, Giovanni Coccapani, Gabriello Ughi, Cosimo Lotti, Matteo Nigetti, Francesco Guadagni and Giulio Parigi. It was the latter's model that captured her fancy. Maria Maddalena decided to give the new villa the name of *Poggio Imperiale* ("Imperial Heights") and to make it the residence of the Grand Duchesses of Tuscany.

Parigi's design yielded a central building flanked by two lower, symmetrical wings with terraces and semicircular concave profiles that circumscribed the vast piazza in front of the rather uninteresting main façade.

The enveloping wings and semicircular balustrades encircling the piazza were situated at the end of a straight, ascending avenue lined with holm oaks and cypresses, which began at Porta Romana amidst a grandiose arrangement of four statues and four pools (removed in 1765). The entrance to the piazza, by contrast, was guarded, at the end of each balustrade, by Vincenzo de' Rossi's Cinquecento statue of Hercules holding up the sky and Felice Palma's Seicento statue of Jove hurling thunderbolts.

Inside the villa, Parigi restructured the old central courtyard and the rooms of the grand-ducal apartment, which were painted in fresco by Matteo Rosselli and his pupils.

After it passed to Grand Duchess Vittoria Della Rovere, wife of Ferdinand II, the building was further enlarged and embellished. Among other things that date from this period were the creation of a ground-floor room "at the head of the courtyard," from plans by Diacinto Maria Marmi, and the redesigning of the courtyard and loggias under the direction of Giovan Battista Foggini.

259

At Villa del Poggio
Imperiale, a room with
paintings of scenes from the
life of Achilles by Domenico
Nani (known as L'Udine),
commissioned by Lorraine
Grand Duke Ferdinando III.

The definitive restructuring of the villa took place during the Lorraine era, spurred by the initiatives of Pietro Leopoldo. The Grand Duke engaged the architect Gaspare Paoletti to build two courtyards alongside the old, central courtyard, effectively doubling the volume of the building, which gradually took up the area of the "orange

Allegorical figures of Agriculture, Sheep-farming, and Commerce, by Giuseppe Fabbrini, in the room at Villa del Poggio Imperiale used as Pietro Leopoldo's Secretariat.

Right: Room of the Biblical Heroines at Villa del Poggio Imperiale. The chamber takes its name from the lunette paintings executed by Matteo Rosselli and his pupils in 1623.

Detail of a grottesche décor by Stefano Catani (1801), on a wall in the Room of the Biblical Heroines.

grove" and the "flower garden."

Paoletti also designed the rear façade and the great ballroom on the *piano nobile*, adorned with the stuccowork of Giocondo and Grato Albertolli. The fresco decoration of the new rooms was assigned to Tommaso

Ceiling of the Audience Room of Maria Maddalena of Austria at Villa del Poggio Imperiale. Depicted in the lunettes are scenes from the lives of holy queens and empresses. At the center of the vault is an allegorical figure of the Holy Roman Empire. The paintings are by Matteo Rosselli.

Gherardini, Giuliano Traballesi, Giuseppe Del Moro, Gian Maria Terreni, Giuseppe Fabbrini, Gesualdo Ferri, Antonio Ciofi, Giuseppe Gricci, and Stefano Amigoli.

Pietro Leopoldo also intended to complete the renovations with a new principal façade, to be designed by Paoletti. As it turned out, however, it was Maria Louisa of Bourbon, Queen of Etruria, who took this initiative. In 1806, she commissioned a plan from Pasquale Poccianti, who managed only to complete the rusticated five-bay portico that was supposed to be flanked by two avant-corps housing a theater and a chapel.

The façade was finally completed by Napoleon's sister Elisa Baciocchi, Princess of Piombino and Lucca and Grand Duchess of Tuscany, who hired Giuseppe Cacialli to execute the rest of Poccianti's design. Cacialli, however, interpreted the plan rather freely, placing atop the rusticated portico a loggia with Ionic half-columns framing arched apertures and supporting a broad pediment. The variants adopted by Cacialli enabled him to add to the *piano nobile* a luminous peristyle with stuccowork and wall paintings.

In 1812, Elisa Baciocchi also commissioned Giuseppe Manetti to draw up plans–later abandoned–for a large "picturesque" garden. With the return of the House of Lorraine in 1814, the avant-corps, serving as a chapel and a guard house, were finally built, and a number of other rooms were decorated by the painters Domenico Nani and Giorgio Angiolini.

In 1865, the villa became a boarding school run by the convent of the Santissima Annunziata.

VILLA RONCIONI
Pugnano, Pisa

RONCIONI
FAMILY

COAT OF ARMS:
Azure a horse rampant argent

In 1468, Antonio di Guelfo Roncioni purchased "a piece of land with farmhouses" at the western foot of Monte Pisano. From these "farmhouses" the descendants of Antonio di Guelfo gradually built the structure that in 1592 was called the "great house."

The transformation of the 16th-century "great house" into a villa took place from 1773 to 1779 upon the initiative of Francesco Roncioni, based on plans by the architect Giuseppe Gaetano Niccolai. These external and internal renovations of the Cinquecento nucleus yielded a building volumetrically characterized by a central mass greater in height than the two blocks flanking it. The smooth, bi-level façade was divided by full-height pilaster strips and embellished, in the middle section, by the customary vertical composition of doorway, balcony, and window with pediment crowned by the family coat of arms.

Far livelier, on the other hand, is the villa's interior, if for no other reason than the illusionistic frescoes that give the central *salone* the airy look of a great arcade with trompe-l'oeil staircases to one side and a faux balustrade on the ceiling, framing an allegorical figure of Spring. These *quadrature* were executed in 1781 by the Neapolitan Pasquale Cioffo, who also painted the *di sotto in su* view of the elaborate colonnade "dissolving" the vault of the stairwell.

Other rooms feature illusionistic frescoes of draperies, merry Bacchic revels viewed beyond trabeated loggias, and fanciful landscapes glimpsed through raised, transparent curtains.

Yet the villa's charm and its ornate rooms suddenly take second place beside the stunning silkworm house with spinning mills, built in 1831 in the adjacent garden from plans by Alessandro Gherardesca. It is

The 18th-century villa, with Monte Pisano in the background.

270

unquestionably a work of singular importance, for it constitutes the first Italian example of the application of Gothic-revival elements to an industrial building typology, and is a rare and impressive specimen of industrial archaeology still intact today.

The silkworm house has the external appearance of a "Gothick" abbey, with terra-cotta statues, mullioned windows, pinnacles, and pointed gables that mask its intended purpose. The silk mill was located on the ground floor, while the silkworm breeding farms were upstairs. This arrangement helped to alleviate work conditions in a situation governed by paternalistic relations.

According to Gherardesca's plan, the

Page 274: At Villa Roncioni, a detail of a mural depicting a Bacchic revel.

Page 275: Bathroom wall decorated with figures in Neoclassical dress, landscapes, and trompe-l'oeil curtains.

Silkworm house and spinning mill at Villa Roncioni, designed in 1826 by the Pisan architect Alessandro Gherardesca and built in the garden.

Below: At Villa Roncioni, a small neo-Gothic church built in 1846 from plans by Gherardesca.

Right: Neoclassical façade of the nymphaeum.

silkworm house was intended to constitute "a majestic setting together with the adjacent wood, the well-tended garden, and the different crops covering the picturesque slopes of the hill." In this graceful and Romantic framework of greenery the architect also inserted a little church, a hermitage, and a nymphaeum.

For the façade of the church built in 1846, Gherardesca once again resorted to neo-medieval forms, actually reassembling the fragments of an authentic Gothic triforium on the pointed gable. For the nymphaeum, on the other hand, he chose a solution combining two styles. The exterior features a Neoclassical composition of half-columns and statues that give a triumphal accent to the great arched entrance. The interior, on the other hand, presents a neo-Mannerist repertory of decorations made up of natural and artificial encrustations, rough-hewn mosaics, and small marble fountains in the form of shells, with derisive masks above that spouted water from their mouths.

Interior of the 19th-century
nymphaeum at Villa
Roncioni, with vault and
walls decorated in a rustic
style inspired by grottoes of
the Mannerist period.

VILLA NAPOLEON-DEMIDOFF
Portoferraio, Isle of Elba

NAPOLEON

The house of the Mulini and the Villa di San Martino at Portoferraio served as the modest but dignified dwellings of Napoleon during his brief stay in exile on the island of Elba (1814-15).

The little villa, which was created from an earlier farm building, has two stories. The lower floor contains the service quarters and "Paolina's bath," which features wall paintings with illusionistic weaves of climbing plants against a background of dark sky.

The upper story, on the other hand, was equipped for receptions and as a residence that included the dignitaries of the small court. Here, at the center of the planimetric square, is the Egyptian Room, which with its frescoes–faux bas-reliefs of hieroglyphs and an illusionistic open gallery looking out on

exotic landscapes–nostalgically recalled the happier, more glorious times of military conquest and Imperial venture. The trompe-l'oeil painting of hanging curtains in the Emperor's apartment seems likewise to allude to the elegant interior of a field tent.

After a period of neglect, the Villa di San Martino was acquired in 1851 by Prince Anatole Demidoff, a relative of the Bonapartes. The prince's intention was to use it to house a collection of Napoleonic memorabilia, and with this goal in mind he hired the architect Nicola Matas to design a grandiose museum that would actually incorporate the villa.

Matas's building, a horizontally developed structure on an axis with the villa, which sits on an embankment behind it, functions as a monumental basement and propylaeum–that is, as an appropriate transition and solemn entrance to the villa-relic. The stateliness of this temple-like pavilion, with its pronaos, projecting wings, and Neoclassical architecture and ornamentation (metopes, triglyphs, eagles), seems well suited to the celebration of the Napoleonic myth.

Completed in 1856 and opened to the public three years later, the museum featured paintings and engravings by Vernet and Gérard, busts of Napoleon family members, manuscripts, ceramics, bronzes, and Canova's marble statue of Letizia Bonaparte. A mere twenty years later, the collection of mementos was sold at auction by Anatole Demidoff's grandson.

Detail of the basement of the museum building erected by Prince Anatole Demidoff.

The museum structure, built as a monumental propylaeum to the Villa di San Martino, where Napoleon stayed during his exile.

281

Right: Reception room at Villa Napoleon-Demidoff, with central basin-fountain and Egyptian-revival wall paintings. The signs of the Zodiac are depicted on the ceiling.

Below: The illusionistic colonnade on the walls here frames a view of an Arab encampment.

VILLA DI SANMEZZANO
Rignano sull'Arno, Florence

In the intradoses of the horseshoe arches of the Moorish vestibule to this villa (acquired in 1605 by the Ximenes d'Aragona family and bequeathed to the Panciatichi in 1816) are inscribed the words: "This room was conceived and executed by Marquess Ferdinando Panciatichi Ximenes d'Aragona, in the year of Our Lord 1853." Thus did Panciatichi, in the dual role of architect and patron, leave his signature on one of the first elements of his stunning monument, proudly displaying on the wall for all to see the motto *Non plus ultra*. Indeed, it is difficult to imagine anything that might compare with his extraordinary Tuscan Alhambra.

To make clear the sentimental and cultural motives that led the Marquess to create rooms even more fanciful and

Rear façade of the villa.

285

Details of décor in the
Fleur-de-lis Room.

glittering than those of his Granadian model, he saw fit to write on one of the walls of the octagonal White Room: "Proud blood of Aragon flows in my veins." And to explain his choice of forms, in the magical Lovers' Room he wrote: "The occult charms of a fantastic style were revealed to me by a benevolent fairy."

The four epigraphs refer explicitly to the ideas informing Panciatichi's project: invention, exceptionality of result, Romantic exaltation of cultural and family origins, and fantastic style. The Alhambra of Sanmezzano is the concrete, successful translation of these guiding principles into architecture.

As we have seen, the first documentation of Ferdinando's neo-Moorish renovations is dated 1853. The White Room was built ten years later, in 1863, and the Gallery between the Room of Mirrors and the octagonal Smoking Room, in 1870. Other rooms followed in a crescendo of execution: the Peacock Room, the Fleur-de-lis Room, the Stalactite Room, the Room of the Spanish Bowls, and the Lovers' Room (where, in gold lettering, are written the names Clorinda, Tancredi, Erminia, Rinaldo, Armida, Lancelot, Guinevere, Bradamante, Orlando, Angelica, Medoro, Ruggero, Tristan, and Isolde).

In these vast, interconnected spaces, teeming with niches, hidden nooks, openings, balconies, rows of columns, and labyrinthine corridors, lives a fantasy of endless corbels, capitals, arches, portals, fan vaults, domes, and pendentives dripping with tracery. The interior constitutes a reverie of walls covered with plaster arabesques and vibrant multicolor *azulejos*, with botanic and geometric interlacing in the *mudejar* style and even Plateresque excesses.

Ferdinando Panciatichi used the Moorish

The dazzling Peacock Room at Villa di Sanmezzano. The shape of the peacock's tail is echoed by the fan vaulting.

East to inspire himself and others to dream, to commemorate and mythify the civilization of his family's origins, and to give the villa an enchanted, recreational aspect that for all its stylistic peculiarities could still be adapted to the functional and typological requirements of Western-style dwellings. So convinced was Panciatichi of this adaptability, and so firmly did he believe in the evocative powers of these Arabian Night settings, that he continued to use the Moorish style (and to publish articles about it from 1879 to 1885 in the Florentine review *Ricordi di Architettura*) in designing the "Guard house in the park of Sanmezzano," the "Gatehouse of a park," the "Two-room interiors," and the quasi-oneiric "Rich Oriental cenotaph."

After 1873 the overwhelming, ingenious revisitation of the East, whose splendor had till then been limited to the villa's interiors, suddenly burst forth on the outside as well, culminating in the addition of the entrance tower in 1889, with its triumphal ogee arch and two onion-domed mini-pagodas at the corners.

The surface of the rest of the façade–bordered at the top with brick antefixes in the Moorish style–was decorated with brick stringcourse fasciae that link up with the window frames and lozenge motifs between the top-floor windows. This ornamentation, which continues on both sides of the building and on the rear façade–the latter distinguished by a broad semicircular gable–are also in the style that Panciatichi held so dear.

Opposite: At Villa di Sanmezzano, the Lovers' Room, commemorating the heroes and heroines of chivalric legend.

Below: Octagonal Room of the Spanish Bowls, so called for the round ceramic medallions set in the colored stuccowork of the vault.

At Villa di Sanmezzano, the gallery and loggia of the circular, central White Room, completed in 1863. The domed ceiling is covered with tracery in stucco.

VILLA OPPENHEIM-CORA
Florence

In 1870-71, the financier Gustavo Oppenheim (who had assets and concerns in Egypt) had this massive villa erected from plans by Giuseppe Comparini Rossi. It was built on a plot of land that the architect Giuseppe Poggi (with whom Rossi worked) had meant, in his urban planning, to become a kind of coronation of the upscale Viale dei Colli. The scheme would have provided a panoramic complement of the projected enlargement of Florence, the short-lived capital of the new Italian republic. For Oppenheim it was to be a symbol of the status he had attained.

On the main façade, the slight projection of the middle section–which features two rows of three windows, framed by arches on the ground floor and by columns above–gives some life to the building's cubic mass. The formal organization of this section (like the repetitive treatment of the other façades) is somewhat unimaginatively drawn from the sober Cinquecento rhetoric that Poggi adopted for the south front of Villa Favard, also in Florence. The building, moreover, utterly lacks any sort of salient element with broad apertures that might afford a view of the appealing cityscape outside.

Behind the monotony of the outside walls, however, the villa's interior has a surprise. Its fancifully decorated rooms reflect a then avant-garde eclecticism given to flaunting a vast formal repertory that included the exotic. Clearly Oppenheim must have thought the drab, boxy house designed by Comparini needed some sort of healthy aesthetic transgressions to enliven it.

To the wide range of disparate revival styles are due, among other things, the neo-Pompeian vestibules, a neo-Moorish sitting room, a neo-Byzantine room, and a neo-Rococo *salone*. All of them were conceived by the open-minded Turin engineer Edoardo

The exterior of the villa is indebted to a severe Cinquecento style.

A flower painting by Luigi Samoggia, on the ballroom ceiling in Villa Oppenheim-Cora.

Gioja, a veteran of the Suez Canal project whom Oppenheimer engaged to satisfy his taste for ostentation with the appropriate décor.

The rich and varied interior decorations were executed in 1872 by a group of Florentine painters, sculptors, and craftsmen. Their number included Ernesto Bellandi, who painted the *Allegories* of scientific and economic progress on the ceiling of the foyer; Augusto Passaglia, who carved the tender figure of the girl on the mantelpiece in one of the sitting rooms; Antonio Quadri, who made the silver-plated bas-reliefs on the ballroom's vaulted ceiling; Orazio Pucci and Bernardo and Nicola Ramelli, authors of the fine stuccowork; and Francesco Morini, who together with the Barbetti brothers made and inlaid both furniture and doors.

Yet the most original and "modern" of the villa's aesthetic delights are clearly the floral compositions of the Bolognese Luigi Samoggia, the exquisitely colored *Cupid and Psyche* of the Milanese Angelo Pietrasanta (which adorns the center of the ballroom ceiling), and the blue and gold, arabesqued dome of the Moorish sitting room, painted by Antonio Caremmi.

Complementing the sumptuous décor are polychrome marble and parquet floors, variously arched and sculpted door and window frames, mantelpieces of white Carrara marble or black stone with semiprecious inlays, and both chandeliers and sconces of blown and colored glass.

The villa, however, was abandoned by the Oppenheims after only a few years, owing to family discord and financial problems. In 1894, it was bought by Egidio Cora.

Overleaf: Rotunda decorated with stuccowork in Villa Oppenheim-Cora. The vault contains allegorical paintings by Ernesto Bellandi. The statue of the dancing maiden in the middle is the work of Francesco Barzaghi.

Page 299: Ceiling of a ground-floor room, with paintings by Luigi Samoggia. The figure in the foreground was carved by Augusto Passaglia.

Detail of Carrara-marble mantelpiece in a ground-floor sitting room, sensitively carved by Augusto Passaglia.

VILLA STIBBERT
Florence

STIBBERT
FAMILY

Starting in 1880, the Scotsman Frederick Stibbert, a shareholder in the East India Company and a former comrade-in-arms of Garibaldi, began to assemble the various building elements that would make up his residence on the Montughi hill. The new structure was erected on land previously occupied by two old country houses belonging to the Davanzati family, one of which was torn down; the other, which had been renovated in the early 1800s by the Mazzeri, was incorporated into the new villa.

For the planning and supervision of his project, Stibbert turned to the architect Gaetano Fortini, while the various interior decorations were assigned to the painters Gaetano Bianchi and Annibale Gatti, the sculptor Augusto Passaglia, and the decorator Michele Piovano.

The multiple building phases led to the creation of an eclectic "castle" combining a number of revival styles: a suitable framework for incorporating sundry antique items (such as the Venetian ogival *loggetta*, reassembled by Tito Bellini to form a small courtyard) and for housing, in a fairy-tale setting, Stibbert's extraordinary collections of arms and armor (European and Middle and Far Eastern), period furniture, paintings, Quattrocento *cassoni* (wedding chests), fabrics, clothing, musical instruments, porcelains, tapestries, medals, plaquettes, snuffboxes, clocks, and small bronzes. The typological assortment of the villa's interconnected sections includes a crenelated tower, a loggia, and a polygonal turret, as well as the surviving bedroom of the previous villa, with Neoclassical frescoes by Ademollo, commissioned by the Mazzeri family. The hybrid façades are covered with coats of arms or charmingly punctuated with little rose windows, niches, marble fragments, mullion windows, stained glass, balustrades, ceramics (modeled on old ones by the Manifattura Cantagalli), and reproductions of Della Robbia *tondi*.

All this variety is then echoed formally and chromatically in Giuseppe Poggi's

Opposite: Venetian wellhead and loggetta reassembled on a terrace of the villa, looking out onto the garden.

Below: The eclectic compendium of the villa's component parts, seen from the garden.

lemon-house, the round, domed chapel designed by Telemaco Buonajuti, and the Egyptian-revival temple (its entrance stairs guarded by terracotta sphinxes and lions) at the edge of the artificial lake, which was installed in the lower reaches of the park under the general supervision of the engineer Gerolamo Passeri. Reflected romantically in the lake's still waters, this imitation temple, a reminder of the timelessness of esoteric and mythic rituals and the seeming destination of an initiatory

*Right: The Malachite Room
in Villa Stibbert, with
Flemish tapestries and rare
15th- and 16th-century suits
of armor. In the middle of
the room is a malachite
table, with gilt bronzes by
Philippe Thomire. Made of
a single block of malachite,
and exceptional for this
reason, the table belonged
to the Demidoff family
before Stibbert acquired it
in 1880.*

journey, is an expression of Stibbert's masonic bent, which also led him to join the venerable Florentine lodge, La Concordia, in 1865.

An amateur painter and photographer, Stibbert gave vent to his artistic and aesthetic tastes–not only on the villa's exterior but also in the teeming neo-medieval, neo-Renaissance, and exotic rooms he created, with sometimes odd scenic effects–in order to house within a sufficiently imaginative setting the perhaps excessive number of objects in his collection (over 50,000 pieces in all). Among the more striking of these rooms are the evocative great Hall of the Cavalcade, with its impressive procession of mounted warriors, foot soldiers, and solemn, caparisoned wooden horses; the Malachite Room, where whole suits of armor and corselets are lined up along the walls like so many manikins; the gallery room, encircled by other ghostly metallic inhabitants, suits of armor for tournaments and jousting, burgonet helmets and various other kinds of headgear, swords, and halberds; the "Japanese" rooms, filled with helmets, terrifying masks, swords, daggers, Samurai shields, and appendages to Mandarin uniforms; the "Moorish" room, filled with a smaller "cavalcade" and breastplates from Turkey, India, Persia, and the Caucasus; the Empire Lodge; and the ballroom.

Together these rooms form a fascinating, museum-like continuum that communicates directly with the spaces reserved specifically for living. Stibbert's intentions in conceiving them no doubt included that of evoking and glorifying the legendary warriors of times past, with whom he clearly liked to identify himself and whose roles, perhaps, he could even have wished to re-enact.

In 1906, upon his death, Stibbert

*Page 304: The Hall of the
Cavalcade at Villa Stibbert
features an impressive
array of fourteen knights
and fourteen foot soldiers
of the 16th century,
accoutred with original
arms and armor from Italy,
Spain, Germany, and the
Middle East. The
picturesque assembly
evokes the atmosphere of a
cavalcade of the period.
The decorative wall
paintings are by Gaetano
Bisuchi.*

Dining room at Villa Stibbert. On the walls hang still lifes of the Neapolitan school and portraits by Venetian and Florentine painters. All the furniture is from the 19th century, except for a rare Italian 18th-century spinet with a painting of Orpheus screnading animals.

At Villa Stibbert, a bedroom with a boat bed made in the 19th century by Italian craftsmen from a French model. On the walls are paintings of Classical subjects by Luigi Ademollo.

bequeathed the villa (the construction of which had continued up to 1901) and its contents–the fruit of passionate and sophisticated collecting–to "the British Nation." The British government, however, sensitive to the pressing requests coming from Florence, found it best to donate Stibbert's estate to the city. Thus in 1909, the Stibbert Museum was opened to the public.

Neo Egyptian temple on the grounds of Villa Stibbert.

VILLA PUCCINI
Torre del Lago, Lucca

Opposite: A corner of the sitting room and study. On the far wall is a portrait of Puccini by Giacomo Grosso.

Below: The sitting-room fireplace, with an Art Nouveau ceramic panel above it by Galileo Chini.

When, in 1891, Giacomo Puccini rented the house of the gamekeeper Venanzio Barsuglia–which was to become his favorite retreat–it still belonged to the Archdukes of Austria and practically bordered on the waters and reed thickets of Lake Massaciuccoli. In 1896, the composer's quest for a quiet, secluded place, as well as his passion for wildfowling, convinced him to buy the house (which included a tower) with the considerable material gains he enjoyed from the success of *La Bohème*, and to refurbish it in a tasteful bourgeois style.

In order to create a little garden behind the house, Puccini asked and obtained permission to fill up a small part of the lake from its owners, the Marquess Ginori family.

Drawn by the composer's charismatic presence and his pleasure-loving, generous way of life, an "artistic and merry-making coterie" formed around him. It included the painters Ferruccio Pagni, Francesco Fanelli, Angiolo Tommasi, Plinio Nomellini, and Raffaello Gambogi. They would hold their gatherings on the shore of the lake, in a grass hut that they called the "Club della Bohème."

In the peace and quiet of Torre del Lago, surrounded by close friends, Giacomo Puccini found the right emotional stimuli for his work, and gradually the little villa became his preferred place of residence.

The few, modest rooms of the house, which are packed with Puccini mementos, still preserve that appealing atmosphere, part Bohemian, part melancholic, that coddled and protected the composer. The stylistically contrasting furnishings–neo-Renaissance decorations and furniture, Art Nouveau ceramics by Galileo Chini, cabinetwork by Bugatti, Oriental screen, chandeliers, lampshades, and statuettes in various styles–are unmistakable signs of a cultured sensibility still capable of appreciating "good things of bad taste."

In order to accommodate Puccini's tomb in his little villa, a small chapel was built in 1926 by the architect Vincenzo Pilotto. It features two bas-reliefs by Antonio Maraini, and a stained-glass window and mosaic, both designed by Adolfo de Carolis.

MAP OF VILLAS

1. Villa Medici at Careggi, Florence

2. Villa Medici at Poggio a Caiano, Prato

3. Villa Le Volte, Siena

4. Villa La Suvera, Pievescola, Siena

5. Villa di Vicobello, Siena

6. Villa Celsi, Celsa, Siena

7. Villa di Belcaro, Siena

8. Villa Niccolini, Camugliano, Pisa

9. Villa I Collazzi, Giogoli, Florence

10. Villa Medici at Castello, Florence

11. Villa Martelli, Gricigliano, Florence

12. Villa Medici La Petraia, Castello, Florence

13. Villa Pannocchieschi d'Elci, Anqua, Siena

14. Villa di Pratolino, Florence

15. Villa Medici at Artimino, Prato

16. Villa La Gamberaia, Settignano, Florence

17. Villa Garzoni, Collodi, Pistoia

18. Villa Mansi, Segromigno, Lucca

19. Villa Corsi, Sesto Fiorentino, Florence

20. Villa L'Ugolino, Florence

21. Villa Burlamacchi, Gattaiola, Lucca

22. Villa di Celle, Pistoia

23. Villa La Pietra, Florence

24. Villa Chigi, Cetinale, Siena

25. Villa Corsini, Castello, Florence

26. Villa di Lappeggi, Grassina, Florence

27. Villa di Poggio Torselli, San Casciano Val di Pesa, Florence

28. Villa Santini, Camigliano, Lucca

29. Villa Malaspina, Caniparola di Fosdinovo, Massa Carrara

30. Villa La Tana, Candeli, Florence

31. Villa Bianchi Bandinelli, Geggiano, Siena

32. Villa del Poggio Imperiale, Florence

33. Villa Roncioni, Pugnano, Pisa

34. Villa Napoleon-Demidoff, Portoferraio, Isle of Elba

35. Villa di Sanmezzano, Rignano sull'Arno, Florence

36. Villa Oppenheim-Cora, Florence

37. Villa Stibbert, Florence

38. Villa Puccini, Torre del Lago, Lucca

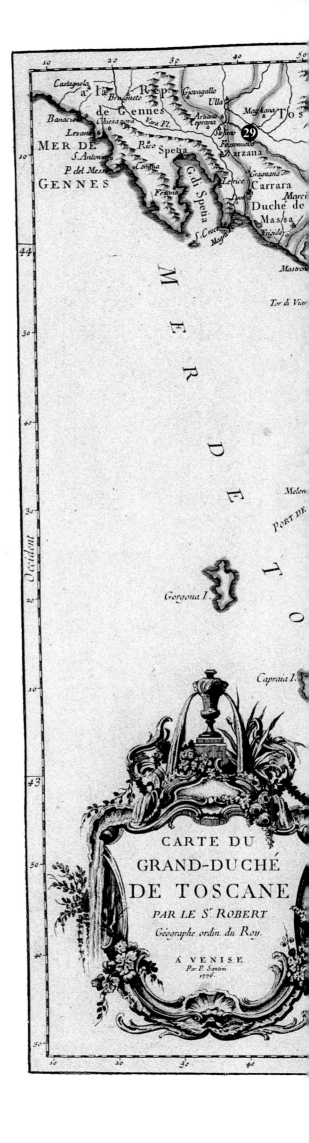

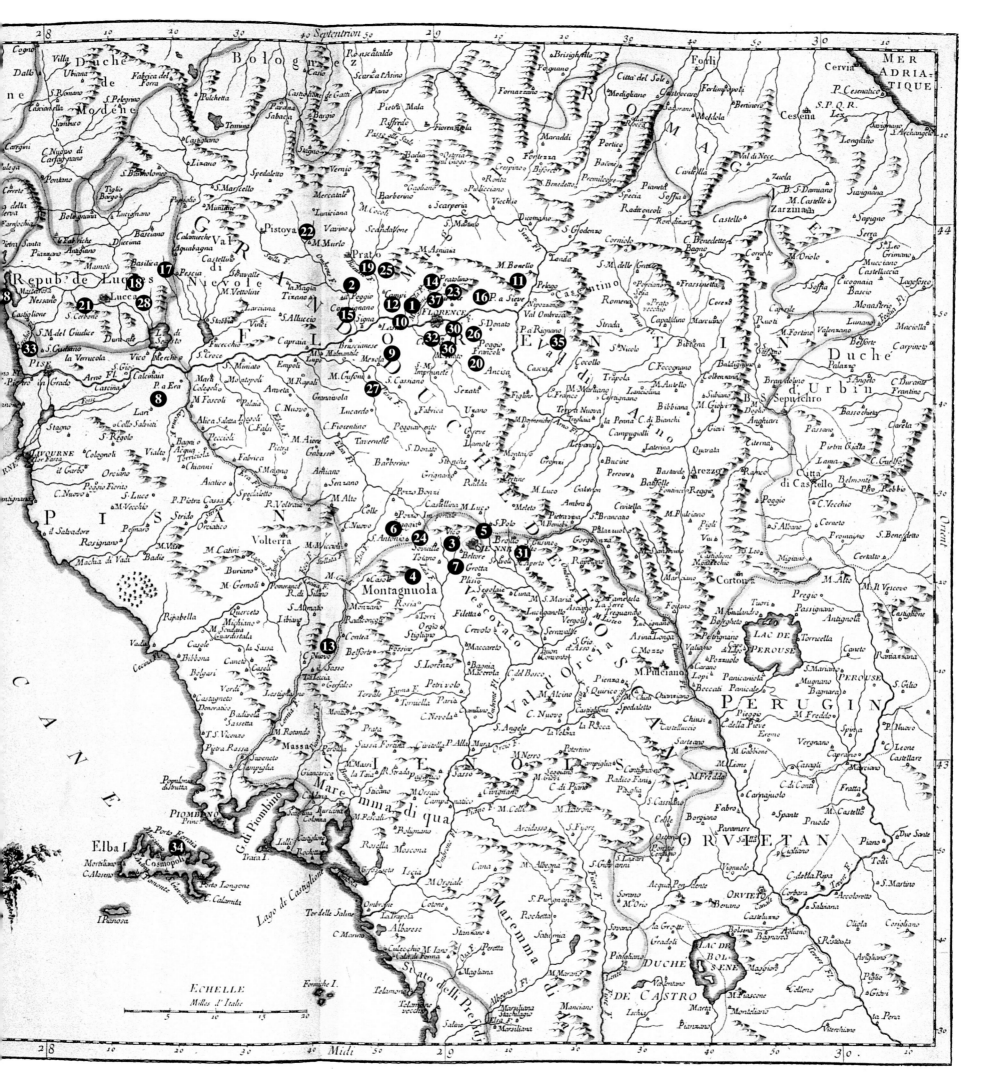

313

BIBLIOGRAPHY

Acidini Luchinat, C. *La grottesca* in *Storia dell'arte italiana: Forme e modelli*. Vol. XI. Turin, 1982; Ackerman, J. *The Villa: Form and Ideology of Country Houses*. Princeton, 1990; Acton, H. *The Last Medici*. London, 1962; Acton, H. *Great Houses of Italy: The Tuscan Villas*. London and New York, 1973; Alberti, L.B. *I libri della Famiglia*. Edited by G. Mancini. Florence, 1908; Alberti, L.B. *Villa* in *Opere volgari*. Edited by C. Grayson. Florence, 1960; Alberti, L.B. *L'architettura (De Re Aedificatoria)*. Edited by G. Orlandi. Milan, 1966; Andreini Galli, N. and F. Gurrieri. *Il giardino e il castello Garzoni a Collodi*. Florence,1975; Andreini Galli, N. *Ville pistoiesi*. Pistoia, 1989; Anguillesi, G. *Notizie storiche dei palazzi e ville appartenenti alla R. Corona di Toscana*. Pisa, 1815; *Architettura e politica da Cosimo I a Ferdinando I*. Edited by G. Spini. Florence, 1976; *Arredi principeschi del Seicento fiorentino: Disegni di Diacinto Maria Manni*. Edited by P. Barocchi and G. Gaeta Bertelà. Turin, 1990; Artom Treves, G. *Anglo-fiorentini di cento anni fa*. 1953; Bagatti, P.F. and S. Lange. *La villa* in *Storia dell'arte italiana: Forme e modelli*. Vol. XI. Turin, 1982; Baldinucci, F. *Notizie de' professori del disegno da Cimabue in qua*. Edited by F. Ranalli. Florence, 1845–1847; Baldinucci, F.S. *Vite di artisti dei secoli XVII–XVIII*. Edited by A. Matteoli. Rome, 1975; Bardazzi, S. and E. Castellani. *La villa medicea di Poggio a Caiano*. Vols. I and II. Prato, 1981; Baroni, G. *Il Castello di Vincigliata e i suoi contorni*. Florence, 1871; Belli, I. *La villa Rossi a Gattaiola*. Lucca, 1956; Belli Barsali, I. *La villa a Lucca dal XV al XIX secolo con una appendice del trattato di G. Saminiati*. Rome, 1964; Belli Barsali, I. *Baldassarre Peruzzi e le ville senesi del Cinquecento*. Siena, 1977; Belli Barsali, I. *Ville e committenti dello Stato di Lucca*. Lucca, 1980; Bellocchi, U. *Le ville di Anton Francesco Doni*. Modena, 1969; Bellotti, G. *La villa dei Collazzi*. Florence, 1893; Berti, L. *Il Principe dello Studiolo: Francesco I dei Medici e la fine del Rinascimento fiorentino*. Florence, 1967; Bianchi Bandinelli, R. *Geggiano*. Edited by M. De Gregorio. Montepulciano, 1985; Bierman, H. "Lo sviluppo della villa toscana sotto l'influenza umanistica della Corte di Lorenzo il Magnifico," *Bollettino C.I.S.A. Andrea Palladio*. XI. Vicenza, 1969; Boccaccio, G. *Decameron*. Translated by M. Musa and P. Bondanella. New York, 1982; Boccia, L.G. *Guida al Museo Stibbert*. Florence, 1983; Borchardt, R. *Città italiane*. Milan, 1989; Borghini, V. *Il riposo*. Edited by M. Rosci. Milan, 1967; Boscarino, S. *Juvarra architetto*. Rome, 1973; Bossaglia, R. and M. Cozzi. *I Coppedè*. Genoa, 1982; Bruni, L. *Panegirico della città di Firenze*. Florence, 1974; Cacialli, G. *Collezione dei disegni di nuove fabbriche e ornati fatti nella R. Villa del Poggio Imperiale*. Florence, 1823; Calvesi, M. *Il sogno di Polifilo prenestino* Rome, 1983; Carocci, G. *La villa medicea di Careggi, memorie e ricordi*. Florence, 1888; Carocci, G. *I dintorni di Firenze*. Vols. I and II. Florence, 1906–1907; Cassarino, E. *La villa medicea di Artimino*. Florence, 1990; Cataneo, P. *I quattro primi libri di architettura*. Venice, 1554; Chastel, A. *Art et humanisme au temps de Laurent le Magnifique: Études sur la Remaissance et le humanisme platonicien*. Paris, 1959; Chatelet Lange, L. "The Grotto of the Unicorn in the Garden of the Villa di Castello," *Art Bulletin*, no. 50 (1968); Chiarini, M. *Artisti alla Corte granducale* (exh. cat.). Florence, 1969; Chiostri, F. *La Petraja, villa e giardino: Settecento anni di storia*. Florence, 1972; Chiostri, F. *Parchi della Toscana*. Todi, 1989; *Città, ville e fortezze della Toscana nel XVIII secolo*. Edited by A. Fara, C. Conforti, and L. Zangheri. Florence, 1978; Conti, G. *Firenze dai Medici ai Lorena: Storia, cronaca aneddotica, costumi: 1670–1737*. Florence, 1909; Cresti, C. and L. Zangheri. *Architetti e ingegneri nella Toscana dell'Ottocento*. Florence, 1978; Cresti, C. *Firenze 1896–1915: La stagione del Liberty*. Florence, 1978; Cresti, C. "Esperienze neogotiche in Toscana," in *Giuseppe Jappelli e il suo tempo*. Padua, 1982; Cresti, C. *Le fontane di Firenze*. Florence, 1982; Cresti, C. *La Toscana dei Lorena: Politica del territorio e architettura*. Milan, 1987; Cresti, C. *L'architettura del Seicento a Firenze*. Rome, 1990; Cruciani Boriosi, M.T. "La realizzazione barocca del giardino italiano e la sua parziale discendenza dalla contemporanea scenografia," *Antichità viva*, no. 4 (1962); Da Bisticci, V. *Vite di uomini illustri del secolo XV*. Florence, 1938; Dami, L. *Il giardino italiano*. Milan, 1924; Dandolo, T. *Panorama di Firenze: La Esposizione Nazionale del 1861 e la villa Demidoff a San Donato*. Milan, 1863; Da Prato, C. *Firenze ai Demidoff. Pratolino e S. Donato, relazione storica e descrittiva*. Florence, 1886; Da Prato, C. *La Torre del Gallo e il suo panorama*. Florence, 1891; Da Prato, C. *La Real villa del Poggio Imperiale*. Florence, 1895; Dati, G. *Istoria di Firenze, dall'anno 1380 all'anno 1405*. Florence, 1735; De Lille, J. *I giardini ossia l'arte di abbellire i paesaggi*. Lucca, 1794; Detti, E. "Una villa di Michelucci," *Illustrazione toscana*, no. 8 (1942); De Vico Fallani, M. *Il Ventaglio: La villa Archinto alle Forbici e il suo parco*. Florence, 1983; De' Vieri, F. *Discorso delle meravigliose opere di Pratolino . . .* Florence, 1586; Diaz, F. *Il Granducato di Toscana. I Medici*. Turin, 1976; Donaldson Eberlein, H. *Villas of Florence and Tuscany*. Philadelphia and London, 1922; Elias, N. *La società di corte*. Bologna, 1980; Fara, A. "Le ville di Bernardo Buontalenti nel tardo Rinascimento toscano," *Storia dell'arte*, no. 29 (1977); Ferrero, G. *Potere: I geni invisibili della città*. Milan, 1981; *Fiorenza in villa*. Florence, 1987; Firpo, L. "La città ideale del Filarete," *Studi in memoria di G. Solari*. Turin, 1954; Foster, P.E. *A Study of Lorenzo de' Medici's Villa at Poggio a Caiano*. New York and London. 1978; Francesco Di Giorgio Martini. *Trattati di architettura, ingegneria e arte militare*. Edited by C. Maltese. Milan, 1967; Franchetti Pardo, V. and G. Casali. *I Medici nel contado fiorentino: Ville e possedimenti agricoli tra Quattrocento e Cinquecento*. Florence, 1978; Ginori Lisci, L. *Cabrei in Toscana: Raccolta di mappe, prospetti e vedute. Sec. XII–sec. XIX*. Florence, 1978; Giusti, M.A. and G. Rasario. *Un itinerario per le ville pisane*. Pisa, 1987; Gobbi, G. *La villa fiorentina: Elementi storici e critici per una lettura*. Florence, 1980; Gori Montanelli, L. *Architettura e paesaggio nella pittura toscana: Dagli inizi alla metà del Quattrocento*. Florence, 1959; Gori Sassoli, M. "Michelozzo e l'architettura di villa nel primo Rinascimento," *Storia dell'arte*, no. 23 (1975); Guicciardini Corsi Salviati, G. *La villa Corsi a Sesto*. Florence, 1937; Hamberg, P.G. "The Villa of Lorenzo il Magnifico at Poggio a Caiano and the Origin of Palladianism," *Idea and Form Studies in the History of Art*. Stockholm, 1959; Hawthorne, N. *The Italian and French Notebooks*. Edited by T. Woodson. Vol. 14 of *The Centenary Edition of the Works of Nathaniel Hawthorne*. Columbus, Ohio, 1980; Heydenreich, L.H. "La villa: genesi e sviluppi fino al Palladio," *Bollettino C.I.S.A. Andrea Palladio*. XI. Vicenza, 1969; *I Riccardi a Firenze e in villa: Tra fasto e cultura* (exh. cat.). Florence, 1983; *Il giardino romantico*. Florence, 1986; *Il giardino storico italiano*. Acts of the Congress. San Quirico d'Orcia, 1978 and Florence, 1981; *Il luogo teatrale a Firenze* (exh. cat.). Edited by M. Fabbri, E. Garbero Zorzi, A.M. Petrioli Tofani, and L. Zorzi. Milan, 1975; Imbert, G. *Seicento fiorentino*. Milan, 1930; *Introduzione ai giardini del Senese* (exh. cat.). Siena, 1976; James, H. *Italian Hours*. London, 1920 ; Kliemann, J.M. *Politische und humanistische Ideen der Medici in der Villa Poggio a Caiano*. Heidelberg, 1976; *La caccia e le arti* (exh. cat.). Florence, 1960; *La città effimera e l'universo artificiale del giardino: La Firenze dei Medici e l'Italia del '500*. Edited by M. Fagiolo. Rome, 1980; Lassels, R. *The Voyage of Italy*. Paris and London, 1670; *La villa lucchese e il suo territorio* (exh. cat.). Florence, 1977; Leader, Scott (Mrs. Lucy E. Baxter). *Vincigliata and Maiano*. London, 1891; Lensi, A. "Ville fiorentine medievali," *Dedalo*, vol. XI. no. 17 (1931); Lensi Orlandi, G. *Le ville di Firenze di qua d'Arno e di là d'Arno*. Vols. I and II. Firenze, 1978; *Le residenze napoleoniche a Portoferraio*. Pisa, 1986; Linaker, A. *Niccolò Puccini, la sua villa di Scornio, i suoi amici*. Pistoia, 1899; *Lorenzo Nottolini architetto a Lucca*. Lucca, 1970; Mannini, M.P. *La decorazione in villa tra Sesto e Castello nel XVI e XVII secolo*. Sesto Fiorentino, 1979; Marchini, G. *Giuliano da Sangallo*. Florence, 1942; Masson, G. *Italian Villas and Palaces*. London, 1959; Masson, G. *Gardens of Italy*. London, 1961; Mastrorocco, M. *Le mutazioni di Proteo: I giardini medicei del Cinquecento*. Florence, 1981; Medri, L. "Un episodio culturale nella villa medicea di Poggio a Caiano: Il teatro di Corte al tempo di Pietro Leopoldo," in *La Toscana dei Lorena: Riforme, territorio, società*. Acts of the Congress of Grosseto. Edited by Z. Ciuffoletti and L. Rombai. Florence, 1989; Mignani, D. *Le ville medicee di Giusto Utens*. Florence, 1980; Mignani, D. "Villeggiature medicee," in *F.M.R.*, no. 1 (1982); Montaigne, M.E. de. *Works . . . Comprising His Essays, Journey into Italy . . .* Edited by W. Hazlitt, revision edited by O.W. Wright. Vol. 4. Boston; *Monumenti del giardino Puccini*. Edited by P. Contrucci. Pistoia, 1845; *Monumenti d'Italia: Ville e giardini*. Edited by F. Borsi. Novara, 1984; Moretti, I. "Case da signore e case da lavorator nelle campagne toscane dell'età comunale," in *Incontri pistoiesi di storia, arte, cultura*. 1986; Morisani, O. *Michelozzo architetto*. Turin, 1951; Morolli, G. *Firenze e il Classicismo: un rapporto difficile*. Florence, 1988; Mosco, M. "La quadreria di Pomona," *F.M.R.*, no. 86 (1991); Mosco, M. and S. Meloni Trkulja. *Natura viva in casa Medici* (exh. cat.). Florence, 1985; Mosco, M., and M. Rizzotto. *Floralia, fluorilegio delle collezioni fiorentine del Sei-Settecento* (exh. cat.). Florence, 1988; Muntz, E. *Precursori e propugnatori del Rinascimento*. Florence, 1920; Palagi, G. *La villa di Lappeggi e il poeta G.B. Fagioli*. Florence, 1876; Papini, A. *Maiano, Vincigliata, Settignano*. Florence, 1876; Passerini, L. *Degli Orti Oricellari: memorie storiche*. Florence, 1854; Patzak, B. *Die Renaissance- und Barockvilla in Italien*. Leipzig, 1908–1913; Petrucci, F. and A. Paolucci. "I Feroni a Bellavista: un esempio di villa barocca in Toscana," *Paragone Arte*, no. 345 (1978); Pieraccini, G. *La stirpe de' Medici di Cafaggiolo*. Florence, 1947; Pietro Leopoldo d'Asburgo Lorena. *Relazioni sul governo della Toscana*. Edited by A. Salvestrini. Vols. I, II, and III. Florence, 1969; Pliny the Younger. *Lettere ai familiari*. Books I–IV. Edited by G. Vitali. Bologna, 1988; *Pratolino, Villa Demidoff: Storia, Arte, Natura*. Edited by Z. Ciuffoletti. Florence, 1990; Recchi, M. "La villa e il giardino nel concetto della Rinascenza italiana," *La critica d'arte*, vol. II. no. 3, issue 9 (1937); Repetti, E. *Dizionario geografico-fisico-storico della Toscana*. Florence, 1833–1846; Rilke, R.M. *Il diario fiorentino*. Milan, 1990; Ronconi, I. *Dizionario d'agricoltura o sia la coltivazione italiana*. Vols. I, III, and IV. Venice, 1783; Rosa, G. *La decorazione dell'età barocca*. Milan, 1966; Ross, J. *Florentine Villas*. London, 1901; Rubinstein, N. *The Government of Florence under the Medici (1434–1494)*. Oxford, 1966; Rudolph, S. "Mecenati a Firenze tra Sei e Settecento: I committenti private," *Arte illustrata*, no. 49 (1972); Rudolph, S. "Mecenati a Firenze tra Sei e Settecento: Aspetti dello stile Cosimo III," *Arte illustrata*, no. 54 (1973); Rudolph, S. "Mecenati a Firenze fra Sei e Settecento: Le opera," *Arte illustrata*, no. 59 (1974); Ruskin, J. *Works*. Edited by E.T. Cook and A. Wedderbrim. 39 Vols. London, 1903–1912: Saminiati, G. "Dell'edificare delle case e palazzi in villa e dell'ordine de' giardini e orti," in I. Belli Barsali, *La villa a Lucca dal XV al XIX secolo*. Rome, 1964; Sbarra, F. *Le pompe di Collodi, deliziosissima villa del Signor Cavalier Romano Garzoni*. Lucca, 1652; Scotti. "Giardini fiorentini e torinesi fra '500 e '600, loro struttura e significato," *L'arte*, no. 6 (1969); Sereni, E. *Storia del paesaggio agrario italiano*. Bari, 1962; Sgrilli, B.S. *Descrizione della Regia Villa, Fontane e Fabbriche di Pratolino*. Florence, 1742; Shepherd, J.C. and G.A. Jellicoe. *Italian Gardens of the Renaissance*. London, 1925; Solerti, A. *Musica, Ballo e Drammatica alla Corte Medicea dal 1600 al 1637*. Florence, 1905; Stiavelli, C. *L'arte in Val di Nievole*. Florence, 1905; Strocchi, M.L. "Bartolomeo Bimbi pittore naturalista alla corte di Cosimo III dei Medici," in *Agrumi, frutta e uve nella Firenze di Bartolomeo Bimbi pittore mediceo*. Florence, 1982; Strocchi, M.L. "Vicende delle ville tra Medici e Lorena," in *La città degli Uffizi* (exh. cat.). Florence, 1982; Tafuri, M. "Il mito naturalistico nell'architettura del '500," *L'arte*, no. 1 (1968); Tenenti, A. *Firenze dal Comune a Lorenzo il Magnifico*. Milan, 1970; Tonelli, M.C. *Testimonianze neomedievali a Firenze* (exh. cat.). Florence, 1980; Tonelli, M.C. "Alhambra anastatica," *F.M.R.*, no. 4 (1982); Torrigiani, L. *Descrizione delle ville di Quinto, Panna e Camigliano*. Florence, 1889; Vasari, G. *Le vite de' più eccellenti Pittori, Scultori ed Architettori . . .* Edited by G. Milanesi. Firenze, 1906; Vasic Vatovec, C. *L'Ambrogiana, una villa dai Medici ai Lorena*. Florence, 1984; *Villa di Poggio Imperiale: Lavori di restauro e di ordinamento*. Edited by O. Panichi and D. Mignani. Florence, 1975; Villani, G. *Cronica*. Florence, 1847; Weise, G. "*Vitalismo, animismo e panpsichismo e la decorazione nel Cinquecento e nel Seicento*," *Critica d'arte*, no. 36 (1959); Weise, G. "Vitalismo, animismo e panpsichismo e la decorazione nel Cinquecento e nel Seicento," *Critica d'arte*, vol. II, no. 38 (1960); Wharton, E. *Italian Villas and Their Gardens*. New York, 1904; Wright, D. *The Medici Villa at Olmo a Castello: Its History and Iconography*. Princeton, 1976; Zangheri, L. *Pratolino, il giardino delle meraviglie*. Vols. I and II. Florence, 1987; Zangheri, L. *Ville della provincia di Firenze: la città*. Milan, 1989; Zocchi, G. *Vedute delle ville e d'altri luoghi della Toscana*. Florence, 1744.

INDEX

Page numbers in roman type refer to text and those in italics refer to captions.